Architects of Anthropology in India

Architects of Anthropology in India

(Volume IV)

Edited by
Sarthak Sengupta

GYAN

Published by

Gyan Publishing House
5, Ansari Road
Daryaganj, New Delhi-110002
Phone: 011-47034999, 9811692060
E-mail: books@gyanbooks.com

Distribution Network
gyanbooks.com
India, USA, Canada, UK, Australia, France

ISBN: 978-81-212-4927-0 (HB)
First Published, 2024

Printed at: Gyan Press, Delhi.

ARCHITECTS OF ANTHROPOLOGY IN INDIA
Editor: SARTHAK SENGUPTA

Dedicated

in remembrance of

Late Girindra Mohan Sengupta and Pratibha Devi

my maternal grandparents

Contents

Acknowledgements

The editor of *Architects of Anthropology in India* recorded a deep sense of appreciation towards the intellectual existence shown by all the contributors to this volume who responded to our invitation with promptness. All the contributors made sincere efforts to contribute their mite in the form of a write-up within the stipulated date for incorporation in this volume and truly without their kind academic support this compilation would never have been possible.

M/s Gyan Publishing House, New Delhi has earned our sincere appreciation and made us indebted through their initiative in bringing out the volume in the minimum possible time.

I would also like to extend my greetings to Dr Monimugdha Bhuyan of the Department of Anthropology, Dibrugarh University for designing the jacket. Thanks are also due to Dr D. Dutta Das, Dr A. Hallikeri, Prof P. Dasgupta, Dr N. Duary, Dr D. Chatterjee, Prof A.R. Banerjee, Prof R. Khongsdier, Dr M. Bhuyan, and Dr Samrat Sengupta for arranging a few photographs to use in the jacket.

I cannot forget to record my debt to my wife Kaveeta, who helped me a lot at every level of the present venture without once losing her patience, and as usual, she never accepts my thanks. Thanks to my sons Sushruta and Samrat, daughter-in-law Surovee, and grand-daughter Shinjinee for their loving support.

Dibrugarh 08.12.2023 **Sarthak Sengupta**

Preface

In India, anthropology was introduced by Sir William Jones, who established the Royal Asiatic Society of Bengal at Calcutta in 1774 to study Nature and Man. However, the teaching of Anthropology in Indian Universities was introduced at the University of Calcutta in 1918 as part of the curriculum of Ancient History and Culture and as a holistic study of humankind began in the same University in 1920 when it was given the status of an independent subject for study at the post-graduate level leading to a postgraduate degree. Thereafter, a separate Department of Anthropology was established in 1921. The year 2020, thus, marks the glorious completion of a hundred years of teaching Anthropology in India, and such an important landmark calls for remembrance.

What is most striking about the discipline is that it is still deficient in having a documented volume on its history and development. It is a matter of great concern that a hundred-year-old academic discipline at the level of postgraduate teaching, which is devoted to the study of the biological and cultural evolution of human beings covering millions of years, could not reconstruct its history. The doyens of anthropology, how through the utmost devotion to the discipline and their obsession to imprint its huge implication in understanding the life of humans, diligently persisted in teaching and researching anthropology in India that deserve proper documentation highlighting a truthful and interpretive assessment of their contributions. Thus, we decided to celebrate this auspicious occasion by deliberating upon the contributions of the founding stalwarts of the discipline who broke new ground in the field of anthropological research in India. In this treatise, a modest attempt has been made to prepare a repository documenting the life and research contribution.

Presentation of this compilation was possible because of the considerable expenditure of initiative, time, and effort of several eminent contributors who volunteered to write on these doyens. I stand deeply indebted to all scholarly contributors for their academic collaboration, and forbearance.

The first volume of the compilation – *Architects of Anthropology in India* – consists of chapters devoted to the academic life and research contribution of doyens like L.K. Ananta Krishna Iyer, Sarat Chandra Roy, Bhupendranath Dutta, Tarak Chandra Das, N.K. Bose, Verrier Elwin, P.C. Biswas, D.N. Majumdar, Irawati Karve, H.D. Sankalia, Stephen Fuchs, C von Furer Haimendorf, Dharanidhar Sen, M.N. Srinivas, S.C. Dube, N.C. Choudhury, Surajit Chandra Sinha, Indera Pal Singh, Asok K. Ghosh, Gopala Sarana, K.S. Singh, Satadal Dasgupta, Amitabha Basu, D.K. Bhattacharya, and V.C. Channa.

The second volume covers a few more distinguished scholars of anthropology, namely, J.P. Mills, B.S. Guha, K.P. Chattopadhaya, A.K. Mitra, S.S. Sarkar, M.C. Goswami, P.K. Bhowmik, Tulika Sen, H.K. Rakshit, K.S. Mathur, T.C. Sharma, Abhimanyu Sharma, D.N. Majumdar, S.R.K. Chopra, D.P. Mukherjee, R.S. Negi, Biswanath Banerjee, B.M. Das, B.N. Sahay, Priyabala Das, R.M. Sarkar, A.K. Haldar, H.C. Sharma, Surinder Nath, and Abdulla Ali Asraf.

The third volume covers sixteen more distinguished anthropologists who contributed immensely towards anthropological studies in India, namely, Alexander Cunningham, Panchanan Mitra, Prasanta Chandra Mahalanobis, and Dilip Kumar Sen, B.K. Roy Burman, Sushanta Chattopadhyay, Pranab Ganguly, L.P. Vidyathi, Bikash Raychaudhuri, Biman Kumar Das Gupta, Chandra Sekhar Singhrol, Amal Kumar Das, Annada Charan Bhagabati, R.S. Mann, V.K. Srivastava, and Tayenjam Shyamacharan Singh

The distinguished anthropologists whose life and academic contributions are portrayed in this volume are: Ram Charan Das, K. Ishwaran, M.K.A. Siddiqui, Kanti Bhusan Pakrasi, N Subba Reddy, S.C. Tiwari, Amulya Ratan Banerjee, Usha Deka, P.R.G. Mathur, Papia Banerjee, Virendra Nath Misra, Keshari N. Sahay, Aloke Kumar Ghosh, Atul Chandra Bhowmik, Birinchi Kumar Medhi, and Jaydip Sen.

All the write-ups are chronologically arranged as per their year of birth. A similar sequence is also maintained in photographs used in the jacket

I shall consider my efforts to be amply rewarded if this volume in any manner arouses interest and encourages the promising anthropologist of India

Dibrugarh, 08.12.2023 **Sarthak Sengupta**

List of Contributors

Dr Abhisikta Ghosh Roy, Anthropologist, Anthropological Survey of India, Ministry of Culture, Government of India, CGO Complex, Seminary Hills, Nagpur, Maharashtra, India, 440006.

Prof Anup Kumar Kapoor, Former Vice-Chancellor, Jiwaji University, Gwalior and Professor (Retd), Department of Anthropology, University of Delhi, Delhi, India, 110007.

Dr Arpita Mandal Nandi, Principal, Panchla Mahavidyalaya, Raghudevpr, Uluberia, Howrah, West Bengal, India, 711322.

Dr Aruna Hallikeri, Associate Professor, Department of Anthropology, Karnataka College of Arts, Dharwad, Karnataka, India, 580001.

Dr A. R. Sankhyan, Formerly of Anthropological Survey of India, Kolkata, Presently, President Palaeo Research Society and Museum, Ghumarwin (Siwalks), Bilaspur District, Himachal Pradesh, 174021.

Dr Deepanjana Dutta Das, Formerly Associate Professor, Department of Anthropology, Dibrugarh University, Dibrugarh, Assam, 786004.

Dr Diptendu Chatterjee, Associate Professor, Department of Anthropology, University of Calcutta, 35, Bullygunge Circular Road, Kolkata, West Bengal, India, 700019.

Dr Gopal Chandra Mandal, Associate Professor, Department of Anthropology, Bangabasi College, 19 Rajkumar Chakrabarty Sarani, Kolkata, West Bengal, India, 700009.

Dr Indrajit Dasgupta, Administrative Co-ordinator, Archana Sharma Foundation of Calcutta, Kolkata, West Bengal, India.

Dr Monimugdha Bhuyan, Research Officer, Department of Anthropology, Dibrugarh University, Dibrugarh, Assam, 786004.

Prof. M.P. Damodaran, Department of Anthropology, University of Madras, Chepauk Campus, Chennai, Tamil Nadu, India, 600005.

Dr Nabakumar Duary, Assistant Anthropologist (Cultural), Anthropological Survey of India, North East Regional Centre, Mawblei, Madanriting, Shillong, Meghalaya, 793021.

Prof. P. Dash Sharma, Former Professor, Department of Anthropology, Ranchi University, Ranchi, Jharkhand, India, 834008.

Prof. P. K. Misra, Former Professor, Department of Anthropology, North Eastern Hill University, Shillong, Meghalaya and Former National Fellow, ICSSR, J. P. Nagar, Mysuru, India, 570008.

Prof. Sarthak Sengupta, Former Professor, Department of Anthropology, Dibrugarh University, Dibrugarh, Assam, 786004.

Prof. Sekh Rahim Mondal, Former Professor of Anthropology and Sociology, Centre for Himalayan Studies and Professor, Department of Anthropology, University of North Bengal Raja Rammohanpur Siliguri, Darjeeling, West Bengal, India, 734013.

Chapter - 1

Prof. Ram Charan Das: A Man of Stately Personality

Deepanjana Dutta Das

Some multitalented, kind-hearted, honest men in society serve as navigators who can steer the tender boats of one's life in the stormy ocean. Here we can point out Prof. Ram Charan Das, a gentleman of refined habit and manners, a diligent educationist, a dignitary in the field of social and welfare activities, and a staunch follower of Gandhian Philosophy. He was a simple man but had a strong sense of humour who neither wanted publicity nor he was craving for economic gain. By spirit and commitment, he remained a social worker throughout his life.

Prof. Das was the founder and head of the Department of Anthropology at Arya Vidyapeeth College, Guwahati, Assam, and taught anthropology for two decades (1962-1982) before he retired from his service in 1982. He has always lived up to his image of an amicable and adorable gentleman who should have an unprecedented sense of commitment to his duties. He was an active member of the Anthropological Society of Assam, later renamed as Anthropological Society of North-East India. He was not merely an active member of the society but was an enthusiastic and wonderful ally in promoting and popularising the discipline of Anthropology in the region. He became the President of the Society for a couple of years. Prof. Das had a personality of diverse facets. His soft and amiable behaviour endears him to all who come in contact with him. His life journey was a saga of achievement in diverse fields for which he received honour from everywhere.

Prof. Ram Charan Das was born on 30th August 1919 in a well-known joint family in a remote village called Bahari in the Barpeta district of Assam. He was the second son of the Late Manuram Das, who was a trader of great repute, and who was known for his hospitality and generosity. His mother Late Felanipriya Das was a deeply pious, open-hearted, sympathetic woman.

He passed his matriculation examination from Barpeta H.E. School in the year 1939 and his I.Sc Examination in 1942 from the Cotton College, Guwahati. However, he lost one year in 1942 for the Quit India Movement. He graduated from St. Pauls' College, Calcutta in 1945. In 1947, he passed his M.A. in Anthropology from Calcutta University. After that, he went to Bombay to complete his Post Graduate Diploma in Social Science Administration from Tata Institute of Social Science in 1950. He proved himself to be a brilliant student by receiving scholarships for the proposals. His passion for higher education enabled him to cross the hurdles on his way to achieving the desired destination. After finishing his education at Calcutta University and Tata Institute of Social Sciences, Mumbai, he met for the first time, the Late B.K. Bhandari is a devoted social worker and the founder of the Assam Seva Samiti, which was founded in 1952. In his lifetime he did a variety of works. But he always remained committed only to his overpowering passion i.e. Social Service. In 1951, he worked as Assistant Secretary of Indian Council of Social Welfare, West Bengal Branch, Calcutta. He undertook earthquake relief and rehabilitation works in North Lakhimpur as a member of Service Civil International i.e. a voluntary organisation. He gathered his experience as a worker as well as an administrator of various capacities at the NGOs' of State, National, and International levels.

In 1953, he joined 'The Assam Seva Samiti' which was at that time in its nascent stage having been founded only in 1952 as a General Secretary for 9 long years he devoted all his time to serving the poor, setting up homes at various places under the aegis of Assam Seva Samiti. This period can rightly be described as a high peak in the graph of social work rendered by Prof. Das. His Anthropological background and psychic setting as a real Anthropologist encouraged him to do welfare activities among the downtrodden section of the people of society. Prof. Das also served as Honorary General Secretary of the Indian Council of Child Welfare, Assam Branch in 1985 for 3 years.

He also served as Honorary Secretary, All Assam Leprosy Association, who were considered untouchables at that time. The most outstanding achievement of Assam Seva Samiti is in the field of eradication of Leprosy and in facilitating treatment of the lepers. This work was mostly conducted amongst the different tribal communities of North East India. Another major initiative of Samiti under Prof. Das's leadership was the establishment of a good number of labour welfare centers for the welfare of the labour employees in the tea industry in particular. The third initiative of the Samiti, under his leadership, was the setting of vocational training centers. Their number was smaller but these centers were instrumental in rendering very effective service to the youth. All three initiatives owe a great deal to the dedication and hard work of Prof. Das. He was also associated with many other welfare and social organisations like B.K. Bhandari Vocational Training Institute at Guwahati as Honorary Principal, for long twenty years from 1966 to 1985. He worked hard to shoulder this noble responsibility and thereby trained hundreds of educated unemployed youth to work.

Prof Das by dint of his honesty and sincerity drew the attention of the great social reformers and he was elected as Vice President of the Indian Council of Social Welfare Board, Assam Branch for 3 years in 1985. In 1990, he was elected as Vice President of the Indian Council of Social Welfare in the Hyderabad session. He was also elected as Vice President of the Assam Seva Samiti in 1981 and Secretary of Loka Seva Samiti of the Assam State Branch in 1981.

Despite his busy schedule of work as a social activist, academic administration, and teaching, he wrote a lot of textbooks to the needs of both Higher Secondary students and Undergraduate students of Anthropology in English and Assamese language. Some of his famous books are *Elements of Anthropology. Prarambhik Nritatta* I & II (in Assamese), *An Introduction to Anthropology, Anthropology for Beginners* (Part I & Part II), *Social and Cultural Anthropology, Samajik aru Sanskriti Nritatta* (Assamese) etc. He possessed profound knowledge in English and Assamese which enabled him to write the book '*Write Correct English*' (bi-lingual), thinking about the deficiency of the students to express their minds in a foreign language like English. His books are a source of preliminary information that is very helpful for teachers who teach the subject of Anthropology to beginners.

Prof. Das was the editor of a monthly magazine entitled '*Samaj'* for 3 years from 1956-1958. The title of the magazine shows that it would uphold the social scenario of contemporary societies with special reference to the problems and prospects of downtrodden societies. Besides these, he also wrote several articles in different national and international journals, books, newspapers, etc.

Prof. R.C. Das uses Khadi Dhoti and Panjabi as his normal dress on all occasions. This indicates his passion for the *'Swadeshi'* concept and culture as an indigenous Indian.

Prof. Das was a deep follower of Mahatma Gandhi. In 1942, he participated in the Quit India Movement launched by Gandhiji when he was a student of intermediate class in Cotton College. He is always devoted to the real Gandhism, which he tried to show by rendering service to the downtrodden communities of Assam. He always remained involved with those NGOs who are doing social work at the grassroots level of society.

Prof. Ram Charan Das was a living legend to his students. His sympathetic and co-ordinating attitudes and pleasant companion always delighted his students, colleagues, and staff of the Arya Vidyapeeth College and other educational institutions. His most praiseworthy qualities as a teacher were those, that he could create a congenial atmosphere in the class and could make the students interested in the subject and his kind approach to the students could win over the psychological stamina of the students to be attentive in the class and as such Prof. Das could attain great respect and honour not only from his students but also from the other members of his department. Even after his retirement, he was a frequent visitor to the Anthropology Department and interacted with the students and faculty members of his department.

Prof. Das is a successful man being the compatible husband of distinguished lady Prof. Laksahira Das, a literature, a poetress and a singer of outstanding merit who was born in an economically affluent family. She is an educationist of high excellence who adorned the Head of the Department of Education Department of Gauhati University. They have been blessed with three sons. However, in his enthusiasm for social service, Prof. Das did not neglect the well-being of their children. He took the right care of them and groomed them to pursue their academic career on the right path. Their youngest son Anirban Das is an Engineer, a famous 'Ghajal' singer and a vocalist of extraordinary merit. Prof. Das established the fact that the pursuit of public service need not necessarily mean the neglect of the duty as a head of the household.

Prof. Ram Charan Das loved to work with disabled persons who had to depend completely on others in their day-to-day lives. He was a man of different spirit, attitude, and temperament. He frequently visited the leper asylum, managed by the 'Seva Samiti' as a leading member of the '*Hind Kustha Nibaran Sangha'* and as a secretary of 'The All Assam Leprosy Association', Guwahati, and rendered humanitarian service to the leprosy patients by helping them providing medicines, bandages, and food, etc. His selfless attitude had always been an inspiration to all the members of the association.

Prof. Das was an active social worker. He had a simple, sober, honest, soft-spoken affectionate personality, associated with several socio-cultural organisations of Assam as well as India. A few of them are:

1. Bharatiya Adimjati Sevak Sangha, New Delhi.
2. Hind Kusta Nibaran Sangha, New Delhi.
3. Gandhi Smarak Nidhi, Guwahati.
4. Gandhi Memorial Leprosy Foundation, Wardha.
5. Sarvoday Ashram, Chandmari, Guwahati.
6. Life member of Asom Sahitya Sabha.
7. Kasturba Ashram, Guwahati.
8. Hind Mazdoor Sangha, Assam Branch.
9. Harijan Sevak Sangha, Assam Branch.
10. Assam Sarvodaya Mandal.
11. Uttar Pub Bharat Haridev Sangha, Guwahati.
12. Sarva Seva Sangha, Wardha.
13. Purba Bharati Seva Sangha.

Prof. Ram Charan Das breathed his last on 8th June 2010. His demise has created a real vacuum in the Anthropological Society of

North East India. The state has lost a scholar, an eminent academician, a writer, and a dedicated social activist. We pay homage to this stalwart, who is always very much alive in the heart of his admires, anthropologists, and students of the region.

Chapter - 2

Life and Works of Prof. K. Ishwaran

Aruna Hallikeri

Introduction

Prof. Karigoudar Ishwaran, a pioneer of Anthropology in Karnataka, was born on 1st November 1922 in Hiremallur village in the present-day Haveri district of Karnataka. He was the son of school teacher Channappa Master. Fond of studying, he left for Belagavi to complete his BA and then to Bombay University to complete his Master's in Kannada literature. His command and creativity over the Kannada language led him to publish many of his stories and poems at a very early age. *Vishanimishagalu* (1945), *Halahala* (1947), and *Rajarani Dekho* (1948) are some of his story collections. He was also working as a Kannada lecturer in Hubbali and Solapur. As he mentions in his autobiography, Ishwaran was inspired by Verrier Elwin's work and writings, thus leading him towards anthropology.

With the help of M N Srinivas, an E.E. Evans Pritchard student at Oxford University, Ishwaran found his way to England to pursue studies in Anthropology. He completed a Diploma in Anthropology in 1955 and a B.Litt on Crime and Punishment in Manu's Dharmashastra from Oxford. He went to Leiden, Holland, to complete his MSS (Sociology) degree in 1957 and further completed his D.Litt on *Family Life in the Netherlands*. In 1959, Wrangler D C Pavate, then Vice-Chancellor of Karnatak University Dharwad called Prof. Ishwaran to become the first Head of the Department at the University's Department of Social Anthropology. Ishwaran took charge as head and nourished the Department from 1959 to 1964. He was instrumental in developing the necessary structure, syllabus, and methodology for imparting knowledge to anthropology students. He also imbibed essential 'fieldwork' methodology as part of their syllabus, thus preparing budding anthropologists. He also started the '*International Journal of Comparative Sociology*,' bringing global recognition to himself and the University. In pursuit of further accomplishment, K Ishwaran went to York University in 1964. He was associated with York University till his lifetime (Ishwaran, 1984). He was so fond of India that he used to come every summer to conduct studies at Dharwad. He has published 28 writeups during his lifetime. He died in Dharwad on 23rd June 1998 when he was on a study visit.

Contributions to Anthropology

We can study Ishwaran's contributions to anthropology in three key areas, i.e., family, village studies, and religion. His D.Litt thesis '*Family Life in the Netherlands*' at Leiden was a prime attempt to analyze the Dutch family system, questioned: 'Has the Dutch family changed in its essentials during the process of social change through which Dutch society has been, passing since the beginning of this century?' By essential characters, Ishwaran meant the core functioning of the family, such as reproduction, maintenance, socialisation, and placement, have changed from pre-industrial to industrial times. Through his analysis of kinship ties, family acting as an agent of transmission of values, and family's role in maintaining the 'way of life,' he concluded that Dutch middle-class families have not changed in their core function; relatively minor adaptations are made towards changing circumstances. (Matthews, 1962; Ishwaran, 1960). Ishwaran's experience reviewing the family's social institution prepared his standpoint from where he will examine society and study it. Social change and its acceptance in social institutions was his prime focus.

Once he started his academic career at Karnatak University Dharwad, he was exposed to village studies and received grants from Research Programme Committee of the Planning Commission, Government of India; he started his study at Shivapur village. From 1960 to 1964, he conducted intensive and extended observation and presented his monograph account in three books, *Sivapur: A*

South Indian Village, Tradition and Economy in Village India, and *A Populistic Community and Modernisation in India*. Ishwaran importantly recognised the dynamism in the village structure and its continuity. In the first book of the monograph, as mentioned above, Chapter 6th, Change and Continuity, Ishwaran discusses that the Indian village, especially in the case of Shivapur, has maintained two factors that have kept them historically persistent; one is their adaptability and other their internal consistency. These factors have kept practices like kinship, dressing patterns, craftsmanship, caste frameworks, and others alive with minor adjustments even when ideological, technological, and military invasions have repeated experiences by them.

Continuing the fervor, in his third series, '*A Populistic Community and Modernisation in India*,' Ishwaran introduces the theory of '*Populistic community*' - a theory of populistic modernisation. This model explained the social change emerging in the Indian rural context. Indian villages, though being exposed to urbanisation and modernisation, traditional elements are being modified without destroying the minimum structural continuity. Thus, he provided a model to put forth the issues of social change (Conklin, 1980).

Max Weber had much influence on Ishwaran's writing on religion. A large part of Ishwaran's writings on religion was on Lingayats. In a three-book series, *Religion and Society among the Lingayats of South India* (1983), *Basava and the Lingayat Religion* (1984), and *The Monastic Systems of the Lingayats of South India* (1998), Ishwaran asserted that tradition and modernity are not antithetical to each other, instead can be complimentary to each other. He supplemented this viewpoint through his Lingayat community study. He also brought the uniqueness of the Lingayat religion, such as women's superior position in the Lingayat religion compared to other South-Indian religions.

Conclusion

In his 38 years of anthropological and sociological career, he always had an intuitive hunger to contribute to society through his research and writings. His seed of academic endeavour, the Department of Anthropology at Karnatak University, has bestowed anthropological knowledge to thousands of students and scholars who serve society in different capacities. However, Dr Raghavendra Rao, a political science expert and friend of K Ishwaran, in K Ishwaran's obituary note, points out that Ishwaran was treated as 'an academic outcast, victim of a conspiracy of silence.' Ishwaran's contributions did not seep into our academic textbooks. His viewpoints are vital to understanding the social fabric of society and its rapid change. There is a need to bring Ishwaran to the forefront

Some important research publications

- 1959 *Life in Netherland Family*, Van Keulen, The Hague.
- 1965 *Urban Sociology* (Joint), Asia Publishing House, New York.
- 1966 *Tradition and Economy in Village India*, Routledge, and Kegan Paul, London.
- 1966 *Politics and Social Change*, E.J.Brill, London.
- 1968 *Shivapur: A South Indian Village*, Routledge and Kegan Paul, London.
- 1972 *Change and Continuity in Indian Villages*, Columbia University Press.
- 1976 *The Canadian Family*, Holt, Rinehart and Winston of Canada, Toronto.
- 1977 *A Populistic Community and Modernisation in India*, E.J. Brill, London.
- 1977 *Family, Kinship and Community: A Study of Dutch Canadian*, McGraw-Hill Ryerson, Toronto.
- 1979 *Childhood and Adolescent in Canada*, McGraw Hill Ryerson.
- 1983 *Religion and Society among the Lingayats of South India*, E.J. Brill, London.
- 1990 *Boeing and Bullock Cart: Studies in Change and Continuity in Indian Civilisation,* Chanakya Publishers, Delhi.
- 1992 *Speaking Vasava: Lingayat Religion and Culture in South India*, West View, Colorado.
- 1992 *Family and Marriage: Cross-cultural Perspectives*, Thompson Educational Publication.
- 1999 *Ascetic Culture: Renunciation and Worldly Engagement*, Brill, London.

References

Conklin George, H. 1980. A populistic community and modernisation in India.by K. Ishwaran. *The Journal* of *Asian Studies*, 39, 2: 409–410. doi:10.2307/2054336

Ishwaran, K. 1984. *Valase Hoda Kannadigana Kathe*, Autobiography, Suruchi Publications.

Matthews, E. 1962. K. Ishwaran, Family life in the Netherlands (Book Review) – ProQuest. *International Journal of Comparative Sociology*, 3,3: 165.

Chapter - 3

Prof. Mohammad Khalil Abbas Siddiqui: A Tribute to a Silent Anthropologist in India

Sekh Rahim Mondal

Introduction

Professor M.K.A. Siddiqui, popularly known as Siddiqui Sahib is one of the important architects of Indian Anthropology, who has worked sincerely on various domains of the discipline as a silent researcher. He was a man trained under several veterans of anthropology during his professional careers like B.S. Guha, N.K. Bose, S.C. Sinha, and many others. Siddiqui was known for his remarkable contributions towards conceptual, methodological, and empirical domains in social anthropology as well as sociology and other fields of social sciences. Unfortunately, his works have not reached a wider academic circle, particularly among present-generation budding anthropologists of the country.

This chapter is an attempt to throw some light on the life and works of Professor M.K.A. Siddiqui as a tribute and homage to a lifelong researcher on the occasion of a hundred years of teaching and research in the anthropology of India. The chapter is based on the facts and works of this great scholar and information obtained from his family members, colleagues, and close friends. All those are synthesised with the author's own experience out of his close association with said scholar since the time of his student days.

[2]

Early life and education

Prof. Siddiqui was born on 10 September 1926 in a reputed Muslim family in the village Jamgaon, location in the district of Bhagalpur in Bihar. He died on 23rd July 2022. His ancestors were *Muftis* and family carrying the legacy of freedom fighters as many of his ancestral relations participated in the first win of independence in 1857. The nationalist tradition of his family is reflected in many of his anthropological thinking and writings.

At a very early age, Siddiqui learned Persian and Urdu from his parents and grandparents. Gradually he learned Arabic and read of Holy Quoran from his maternal grandfather, who was an Arabic scholar. He had his primary and secondary school education in Bhagalpur, where from passed Matriculation and Intermediate examinations with good results. For higher education, he moved to Calcutta (now Kolkata) and did his B.A. (Hons.) in Persian Language from the University of Calcutta in 1949 with first division. He obtained an M.A. degree in Urdu Language from the same University with first class and stood first in position. Later he decided to shift from language studies to social sciences. Got an interest in sociology and obtained another M.A. degree in this subject from Bhagalpur University. Finally, he got an interest in human science and achieved a Ph.D. degree in Anthropology from the University of Calcutta in 1973. His Ph.D. thesis was on *Muslims of Calcutta: Aspects of their Social Organisation,* which he carried out under the active supervision of Prof. Surajit Chandra Sinha. This thesis was published in the form of a book and that gave him wider recognition in the academic circle. This pioneering empirical work opened the gate of Muslim Studies in India's urban context from the perspective of anthropology. Siddiqui was such a man whose childhood was spent in rural Bhagalpur but established his name in the metropolis of Calcutta as an expert anthropologist and social scientist in this cosmopolitan city. In this context, it is important to note that his shift from language studies to human or social societies got impetus from Dr B.S. Guha, Prof. N.K. Bose and Prof. S.C. Sinha and many others of Anthropological Survey of India with whom he was working in the said governmental institution.

[3]

Carrier and position

Siddiqui established his name in the field of cultural anthropology, particularly in the field of urban anthropology and the study of marginal communities in rural social contexts. For a long period, he was closely associated with the Anthropological Survey of India (AnSI), which he joined in 1955 and retired in 1987. During his entire professional life at AnSI, he held several important official positions and also worked in charge of many sections of this reputed research institution of the Government of India. For a long time, he was also in charge of Research Fellows working under various research schemes of this prestigious institution.

After his retirement, he got the prestigious award of Senior Fellow from the Indian Council of Social Science Research (ICSSR), New Delhi, in 1988. After completing this assignment, he joined the Asiatic Society as a Research Professor in 1994. After a little break, to the continuation of his academic interests and creative writings, Siddiqui decided to join the Institute of Objective Studies, popularly known as IOS (a Delhi-based Non-Governmental Research Organisation) as its coordinator of the Kolkata chapter in 1995 and continued such position until he was physically active. In IOS he has conducted and completed several national and regional level research projects of great academic significance.

[4]

Awards and felicitations

For innovative research works and creative writings, Siddiqui received several honours and medals. He obtained Silver as well as Gold medals including the award of a Book Grant from the University of Calcutta for best performances in undergraduate and post-graduate examinations. His scholarly works attracted the attention of both Governmental and Non-Governmental Organisations. He was felicitated by the Department of Youth Services, Government of West Bengal. He received the prestigious Lifetime Achievement Award for his significant contributions to social scientific research. It is to be mentioned that he was the anthropologist who received the prestigious

Netaji Award for his devotional research on Hindu-Muslim relations and writings on communal harmony in India. His works and social activities on peace and conflict resolutions received appreciation and recognition from various concerns.

Siddiqui received the very prestigious Shahwalliulluh Award from the Institute of Objective Studies, New Delhi, for field-based research on various segments of the Indian population including the study of Islam and Muslims in India.

[5]

Significant research contribution and writing

Siddiqui was an anthropologist by training and profession and used his scientific knowledge and skills toward continuous research, writing, and publications. He was a brand of scholar in India who has worked on various social groups of Indian Society like tribes, castes, urban groups, and religious minorities. He studied them not in isolation from each other but rather in terms of inter-ethnic and inter-community relations. He is also an expert in urban anthropology and intensively worked on urban groups, associations, institutions, and other agencies with particular reference to the metropolis of Kolkata from a multidimensional perspective.

Study of tribes and peasants

During his prolonged association with the Anthropological Survey of India for over three decades, Siddiqui took up and completed several major and minor research projects. His major works on tribal groups in India need to be noted here. He did intensive field-based research among the *Dudias,* a least-known tribe of Orissa, and published *The Dudiya: A Forgotten Tribes of Orissa* (1970) a fine monograph on this folk community. His study among *Tadvis* of Satpuda Hills appeared as a noted ethnographic account of this little-known community. His works on the in-group and out-group complex among the tribal communities in Orissa is a path-breaking ethnographic account. He is an anthropologist who has worked on the impact of Islam and Muslims among some tribal groups in the country. In this context his works on *Tadvi Bhils* are highly significant through this study he conceptualised the process of Islamisation among the Tribes in India.

Siddiqui has made a very significant comparative study on the material culture of more than fifty tribal groups living in different tribal zones of India. His book on *Hindustan ki Adivasi* (1971) in Urdu was highly popular among scholars and policymakers of his time.

Siddiqui earned his name in tribal studies for his constructive works on acculturation social change and peasant nation among some Indian tribes, which he meticulously examined in the frame of the tribe–caste–peasant continuum organically initiated by his mentor Prof. S.C. Sinha (1984). His conceptual ideas of the in-group and out-group syndrome among tribal groups of India are very useful in understanding tribal-nontribal interactions from the perspectives of dominant-minority relations (1982), which is one of his pioneering theoretical contributions to Indian anthropology. *Bharat ki Adibasi* (in Hindi) is one of his most notable publications on tribal studies in India. His work's impact on Islam and Islamisation among the Tribes of Central and Western India is a pioneering one (1976, 1979).

Focus on urban society

Through his empirical research on various urban social groups of Calcutta, Siddiqui proved himself as a noted urban anthropologist of the country. His works on slum dwellers and marginalised social groups of this metropolitan city are well recognised. He did several field-based studies on the socio-economic lives of the slum dwellers of India's old city with particular reference to their plights and survival strategies. His works on the issues of family planning and family welfare among slums and pavement dwellers of Calcutta have thrown new lights on the life and living of the urban marginalised groups of this city (1966). His intensive study on *Parsi Bagan Busti* from an anthropological perspective was highly appreciated both by academicians and policymakers. His deep knowledge of the social history of Calcutta got recognition among historians and other social scientists. His edited volume *Aspects of Society and Culture in Calcutta* (1982) got appreciation from various corners. His long in-depth empirical research on various ethnic, social, and religious groups living in Calcutta made him an expert anthropologist on the social and cultural profile of the city. *Life in the Slums of Calcutta* is one of his notable publications in urban anthropology.

Focus on minorities

Siddiqui is both nationally and internationally known for his pioneering anthropological (and sociological) works on the Muslim minority in India, with special reference to the city of Calcutta. His works on varied aspects of Muslim life and living patterns are dozens. Several important such works were published as books as edited volumes and as research papers in professional journals. Among his several such works most notable is *Muslims of Calcutta: Aspects of their Social Organisation* (1974), which happens to be the product of his Ph.D. thesis under the supervision of Prof. Surajit Chandra Sinha. This was published in 1979 and thereafter Muslim studies got new trends in the domain of Indian Anthropology. In addition, some of his other notable works are; *Educating a Backward Minority* (1984), *Muslim Educational Uplift: How to Achieve this Goal* (2008), *Muslims in Free India* (1978), *Social and Cultural Empowerment of Muslims* (2009), *Marginal Muslim Communities in India* (2004), *Voluntary Association of Muslims of Calcutta* (2004), *Institutions and Associations of Muslims of Calcutta, Muslims in India* (1997) and *An Encyclopedic Compendium of Muslim Communities in the World* (2011) deserve special mention. His contribution to the Anthropology of religion and the anthropology of Islam is highly significant which he has shown through his precise publication on *Quoran: A Message for All Mankind* (1989). This publication lucidly explains what Islam is as a philosophy of life and significantly contributed towards the growth of Islamic anthropology as a methodological tool for analysis of the theoretical framework and human society. He has also worked on *Some Linguistic Minorities of Calcutta* (1991).

Focus on physical anthropology and prehistoric archaeology

Siddiquis contribution to other subfields of anthropology is also notable. He did an excellent study on the physical anthropology of the Muslim population in Calcutta along with his colleague Dr Mohadeb Prasad Basu of AnSI. His research on *Racial Affinities of the Hindu-Muslim Population in India* (2002) is a significant contribution to the field of physical anthropology. Based on empirical data (both biological and cultural) he opined that the majority of the Muslim population in India is of local origin. Through such studies, he had to prove that the indication and meaning of indigenous for Hindus and foreigners for Muslims have no empirical base and appear to be burdens of political propaganda.

Siddiquis' book on *Manab-ki-Kahani* (1967) in Hindi is a notable contribution to pre-history and archaeological anthropology. This is primarily dealt with the bio-cultural evolution of mankind.

Focus on nation building: Inter-ethnic and inter-community relations

Siddiqui in the latter phase of his active academic life completely devoted to the study of the issues of inter-ethnic, inter-caste, and inter-community relations in India. His studies on *Hindu-Muslim Relations* (1993) and *Inter-Caste and Inter-Community Relationship: Developing Pattern* (1993) from the perspectives of anthropology have given a new light on the nation-building process. In this context, his most notable publications are *National Integrations* (1976), *National Integration through Education* (1984), *Acculturation and Social Change in India* (1989), *Hindu-Muslim Relations* (1993), *Roots of Communalism in India* (1999), *Hindu-Muslim Understanding* (2004), *Muslims in India: Issues and Challenges* (2011) and *Hindus* and *Muslims in India: A Common Destiny*, (2012), *Harmonizing Civilisational Clashes* (2015) are the most important.

Through those studies Siddiqui has tried to explore not only the missing links and existing links between these two most significant socio-religious groups of India but also discover the emergence, the courses, and consequences of communalism in this country (2003), He had the views that the gradual weakling of inter-ethnic and inter-community (inter-religious) relations has its root in western intrusion and colonial policy of divide and rule, which in recent times getting strength for politics of rule and divide backed by post-truth politics. He had the opinion that for nation-building in multi-cultural India, there is a need for a harmonising interfaith clash by way of interfaith dialogues. This he has shown in his publication of *Harmonizing Civilisational Clashes* (2015). His studies and publications on inter-ethnic and inter-community relations are ready references on the issues of peace and conflict .... and policy formation. His research findings have enough scope to restore the communal and national harmony of incredible India. His publication *The Study of Hindu Muslim Relations: A Exercise in Methodology* is eye-opening.

[6]

Contributions to conceptual, theoretical, and methodological domains

Based on exclusive and intensive field studies Siddiqui notably contributed to developing some concepts theoretical frameworks and methodological perspectives of social-cultural analysis in multicultural and plural social contexts of India. These are (i) marginal community, (ii) marginal classes, (iii) Interlocking social relationships, and (iv) Islamisation in tribal society.

Through his study and writing he has developed the term, the concept of marginal community to denote the social group based on some unique attributes like the (a) position of the group in the national scale of socio-economic development, (b) proximity to distance frame the core elements of culture as possed by the dominant group of its community or others living around them, (c) economic impoverishment of the group and (d) presence of conspicuously large content of cultural elements of little traditions in their ways of living. All these, he meticulously noticed in his works on marginal Muslim communities in India, those are located at the bottom of the social ladder concerning their economic condition and social position. The marginal Muslim communities are located at the borderline (margin) of Hindu and Muslim society. It is important to note that the marginal Muslim communities occupy an important position in India's national politics in recent times. They are popularly designated as Pasmada Muslims.

While by marginal clans, Siddiqui indicated the social category or the social segment of those placed at the bottom of social gradation in terms of their socio-economic condition as well as power and position in the social system. The people(s) of the marginal class lack all essential resources for social progress. Thus, they require economic, political, and social empowerment for their social survival. His strategy believed that the people(s) belonging to the marginal community or marginal class are the weakest of weaker sections of the Indian population confronting achieving the benefits of inclusive policies meant for there as prescribed in the Indian constitution.

He needs to be credited for evolving the concept of interlocking social relationships for understanding inter-ethnic and inter-community relations amongst the varied socio-religious groups living in India. According to him social bondages and bindings emerged out of functional relationships between the social groups. The interlocking relationship emerged out of everyday interactions amongst the different occupational, social, and religious groups for each other's necessities for leading everyday lives in a particular socio-special context. His idea of interlocking social relationships speaks about the overlapping social boundaries that act as a social bridge to minimize the social distance amongst the varied groups living in a plural social context.

Siddieuqi significantly contributed to developing the concept of Islamisation among the tribes based on field studies. He was the first anthropologist who noted the impact of Islam and Muslim cultural elements among some tribal groups of Western and Central India. A similar process he also noticed among some tribal groups of Eastern and North-Eastern regions.

Siddiquis' theoretical and methodological frameworks for social-cultural analysis deserve special mention. He had the view that for understanding a socio-religious group the most important is to examine the social structure and social organisation of the concerned society. For this is said necessary to know the micro and macro levels of social segments and the forces that bind those segments together out of social interactions to run the social system. This methodological perspective can be closely noticed in his classical publication. *Muslims of Calcutta: Aspects of their social Organisation* (1974). Through his general studies, he has concluded that Muslims in India have not constituted a homogenous social category, but rather heterogeneous in terms of patterns of culture and ways of living. He has meticulously noted that there exist some caste-like elements in social life among the Muslims in India including the nature of social stratification in their society like their non-Muslim neighbours (1971).

Through his path-breaking works on marginal Muslim communities in India (2004) Siddiqui has evolved the methods of identifying different Muslim groups as marginal in terms of their history of origin, occupational specialisation, nature of economic pursuit elements of local culture, social attributes, and rootedness in local habitat. Based on them he was able to identify about 170 marginal Muslim groups in India and gave a detailed account of 1/7 of them. It is very interesting to note that many of the marginal Muslim groups of the country are now identified by the state as OBC or MOBS.

Siddiquis' most notable methodological contribution to anthropology has been noticed in his works in *Study of Hindu Muslim Relations India: A Multidimensional Approach* (1999). In this research, his focus was not simply on historical contradictions and conflicts between the two communities, but on functional relations and ground realities that have existed between them since historical times. He has shown the ground realities in terms of (a) racial and biological affinities, (b) historical and social background, (c) dialect and language used in occupational specialisations, (d) dress and food habits, (e) kinship system, (f) process of acculturation, (g) rootedness in the regional social and political system and above all (h) inter-locking relationship amongst them for each other's social survival and co-existence. Siddiqui had the opinion that Hindu-Muslim understanding in terms of their interrelationship is the core of the national integration of India and for which commercial harmony is the most essential (1992).

[7]

Legacies and lessons left

Professor Siddiqui left behind a rich contribution to the domain of knowledge in anthropology through his empirical studies on various ethnic, caste, and other social groups of the country. Through his empirical research, he has not only documented and discovered the various facts and findings about the socio-cultural lives of various groups of people in the country, but also developed some notable concepts, approaches, methods, and perspectives of social analysis. His anthropological vision was much timelier and moved ahead than other scholars of his time. He was a strong critique of Western anthropology and sociology (1997).

Carrying the nationalist tradition of his family, he was a strong believer in the social and national integration of India and advocated some fresh approaches for understanding the inter-ethnic and inter-community relations of the country. His devotional works significantly contributed to peace and conflict resolutions in India from anthropological perspectives. That added a new dimension to research in the discipline of anthropology. On hundred years of teaching and research in the anthropology of India, there is a need to re-look at his innovative works under the present context for its further growth in the coming days to make the discipline more relevant to the public interest.

Siddiqui's thoughts, ideas, and works have significantly contributed towards the growth of the disciple, particularly for some need areas of inquiry. Many scholars benefitted from his motivation and support. Siddiqui was a soft-spoken, polite, and humble gentleman. He had a strong personality and unique nature. A scholar of excellence worked with new ideas and vision and motivated many who had contacts and associations with him irrespective of the disciplines. I as one of his close associates since my student days was immensely enriched by his visions and suggestions for my research, teaching, and curriculum development in the discipline. Through this small write-up, I pay my sincere homage to such a silent researcher in the Anthropology of our country.

[8]

Significant publications

So far information available from Professor Siddiqui wrote about 29 books and monographs and nearly 75 research papers. He also produced videographic and documentary films. The most important of them are as follows.

Books and monographs

1970. *The Didayi: A Forgotten Tribe of Orissa,* (Ethnographic Report with two other authors), New Delhi: Govt. of India, pp. 251

1974. *Muslims of Calcutta – A Study in Aspects of their Social Organisation,* Memoir No.36, Calcutta: Anthropological Survey of India, Govt. of India, pp. 144.

1982. *Aspects of Society and Culture in Calcutta* (Ed.), Calcutta: Anthropological Survey of India, Govt. of India, pp. 273.

1984. *Educating a Backward Minority,* Calcutta, Abadi Publication, pp. 136.

1984. *Bharat ki Adibasi* (in Hindi), Calcutta, Anthropological Survey of India, Govt. of India, Language Series-3.

1989. *The Quran: A Message for all Mankind,* Calcutta; Abadi Publication.

1989. *Acculturation and Social Change in India* (Ed.). Calcutta: Anthological Survey of India.

1993. *Hindu-Muslim Relations,* Calcutta: Abadi Publications.

1993. *Inter-Caste and Inter-Community Relationship: Developing Pattern,* New Delhi: Common Wealth Publications, pp. 178.

1997. *Institutions and Associations of the Muslims in Calcutta,* New Delhi: Institute of Objective Studies, pp. 180.

1998. *Muslims in Free India: Their Social Profile and Problems* (Ed.). New Delhi: Institute of Objective Studies.

2002. *Life in the Slums of Calcutta,* New Delhi, Institute of Objective Studies.

1999. *Study of Hindu-Muslim Relations in India: A Multidimensional Approach,* New Delhi: Institute of Objective Studies.

1999. *Roots of Communalism in India,* Calcutta: Abadi Publications.

2004. *Voluntary Associations of the Muslim in Calcutta,* New Delhi: Institute of Objective Studies.

2002. *Racial Affinities of Hindu and Muslim Populations in India,* Kolkata: Institute of Objective Studies.

2004. *Marginal Muslim Communities in India,* New Delhi: Institute of Objective Studies.

2004. *Hindu-Muslim Understanding,* Kolkata: Institute of Objective Studies.

2009. *Social and Cultural Empowerment of Muslims in India,* New Delhi: Institute of Objective Studies.

2008. *Muslim Educational Uplift: How to Achieve this Goal?* New Delhi: Institute of Objective Studies.

2010. *Manab Ki Kahani (*in Hindi), Calcutta: Abadi Publications.

2011. *Muslims in India Issues and Challenges,* Calcutta: Abadi Publications.

2011. *An Encyclopedia Compendium of Muslim Communities in the World* (5 volumes), New Delhi, A Publication of Institute of Objective Studies.

2012. *Hindus and Muslims in India: A Common Destiny,* Calcutta: Abadi Publications.

2015. *Harmonizing Civilisational Clashes,* Calcutta: Abadi Publications.

Research papers

1966. Attitude towards family planning in the slums of Calcutta, *Population Review* (Madras), Vol. 19. No. 2.

1968. The slums of Calcutta: A problem and its solution, *Indian Journal of Social Work* (Bombay), Vol. 29, No. 2.

1969. Life in the slums of Calcutta: Some aspects, *Economic and Political Weekly* (Bombay), Vol. 4, No. 5.

1968. Family planning: The Islamic point of view, in *Family Planning News,* Vol. 9, No. 7.

1971. Caste among the Muslims of Calcutta, S.C. Sinha (Ed.): *Cultural Profile of Calcutta,* Calcutta: Anthropological Study of India, Govt. of India.

1974. Knowledge about Muslims, *Islam, and the Modern Age*, New Delhi, Vol. 5, No. 3.

1982. In-group out-group complex among tribal communities in Orissa, in B.D. Choudhury (Ed.): *Tribal Development: Problems and Prospects,* New Delhi: Inter India Publications.

1982. The Patuas of Calcutta: A study in an identity crisis, in M.K.A. Siddiqui (Edited): *Aspects of Society and Culture in Calcutta,* Calcutta: Anthropological Survey of India, Govt. of India.

1982. The image makers of Kumartuli, (Jointly with P.J.De), in M.K.A. Siddiqui (Ed.): *Aspects of Society and Culture in Calcutta:* Anthropological Survey of India, Govt. of India.

1976. National integration: Some preliminary considerations, *ERA fortnightly Calcutta,* Vol. 1, No. 7.

1976. Islamisation among the tribe of Central and Western India, *Bulletin of the Anthropological Survey of India,* Vol. 25, No. 3 and 4.

1979. The Didayi kinship system, *Bulletin of the Anthropological Survey of India,* Vol. 59, No. 3.

1979. The impact of Islam on tribes of Central India, *Man in India*, Vol. 59, No. 3.

1968. The pavement dwellers of Calcutta, *Struggle Weekly,* [Special Number].

1984. Peasantisation of the Banaras in a village in Adilabad, in S.B. Chakraborti, B.R. Ghosh and A.K. Danda (Eds.): *Agrarian Situation in India,* Calcutta: Anthropological Survey of India, Govt. of India.

1984. National integration through education, *Indian Nation* (Patna), October 7.

1984. Economic life of the Garasia in Rajasthan Village, (Jointly with N.K. Kundu), *Human Science,* Vol. 33, No. 2.

1989. Muslim education in Calcutta, in Iqbal Ansari (Ed.): *Muslim Situation in India,* New Delhi: Sterling Publication.

1990. Science and Muslim society in India, *MAAS Journal of Islamic Science*, Vol. 6, No. 1.

1991. Some linguistic minorities in Calcutta, *Asian Studies,* Vol. 8, No. 1.

1962. A glossary of anthropological terms (English-Urdu), Calcutta, Anthropological Survey of India, Govt. of India.

1973. A review of 'A survey of research in Sociology and Social Anthropology by ICSSR', *Man in India,* Vol. 53, No. 3.

1992. Muslims in India: Some aspects of their inter-relationship with the social environment, in S. Singh (Ed.): *Caste and People,* Anthropological Survey of India and Institute of Ethnography Moscow, New Delhi: Manohar.

1994. The study of Hindu-Muslim relations: An exercise in methodology, *Journal of the Asiatic Society,* Vol. XXX, No. 3.

1997. Western sociology: A critique, *Journal of Objective Studies,* Vol. 4, No. 1.

2008. Communalism: An ignored malady, *The Statesman,* Festival Issue.

1983. *Hindustan Mein Zat-Pat*, (Urdu Translation of Caste in India by J.H. Hutton), New Delhi: Bureau for Promotion of Urdu, Govt. of India.

1995. Social structure of Pakistan, Calcutta: *Encyclopedia Asiatica.*

2011. *An Encyclopedic Compendium of Muslim Communities in the World.* Subtitle – South Asia, Vol. 1, M.K.A. Siddiqui, South East Asia, 2011, Publisher IOS, 2012, Vol. 2 Javed A. Siddiqui. Central Asia, East Asia and Rusia, Vol. 3.

Video film and documentary

A videographic film on *Crafts and Craftsmen in the Slums of Calcutta,* entitled: *FOR Art of Excellence.*

A documentary on *The Muslims of Calcutta,* [in collaboration with the Late Mr. Ain Rasheed Khan], Entitled: *The Seventh Man.*

Chapter - 4

Life and Works of Professor Kanti Bhushan Pakrasi Towards Anthropological Studies in India

Indrajit Dasgupta

Professor Kanti Bhushan Pakrasi, M.Sc., D. Phil. (Sc.), is less known to the anthropological community in India. He was born on 4th December 1926 in the city of Dhaka which belonged to undivided India. The city is now the capital of Bangladesh. Information in detail about his early childhood is not available. Before the independence of India, the family settled in Calcutta, first in Bhowanipur and then in north Calcutta. He passed the Matriculation Examination from Scottish Church Collegiate School and did his graduation from Scottish Church College, Calcutta. Finally, he obtained a D.Phil. (Sc.) degree in Anthropology from the University of Calcutta in 1968.

Professor P. C. Mahalanobis founded the Indian Statistical Institute (ISI), Calcutta in 1931. Professor Mahalanobis also opened a unit called the Anthropometry and Human Genetics Unit in the Institute. At that time he invited Dr Sudhir Ranjan Das, a physicist by profession, to join the Anthropometry and Human Genetics Unit. Prof. Mahalanobis had the intention to do research on Anthropometry and Human Genetics and to develop this unit with the help and cooperation of Prof. S.R. Das. He began his research work on growth studies of children, especially for the determination of age with the technique of X-ray on bones. Later on, he worked on human genetics and growth which brought the reputation of the Institute to the international level.

With the same expectation Prof.Mahalanobis, the founder director of the Indian Statistical Institute, allowed Prof. Pakrasi to join the newly established Anthropometry and Human Genetics Unit in the later years of the 5th decade of the twentieth century.

Thereafter Prof. Pakrasi pursued research in different areas mainly social anthropology. It is interesting to note that although his specialisation was in physical anthropology, he contributed more to social anthropology considering its application for the benefit and welfare of man. He had a deep interest in the areas of research involving sex ratio, demography of the Indian population, female infanticide in India, and growth studies of Bengalee children. He had collaborative research projects with Prof. Amulya Ratan Banerjee of the University of Calcutta. Their joint project yielded pioneering contributions to biosocial studies in India. Their joint publication entitled *Biosocial Studies in India* (1976) is a remarkable contribution to Indian anthropology. A few of the most important books authored by Prof. Pakrasi are *Female Infanticide in India* (1970), *The Uprooted: A Sociological Study of the Refugees of West Bengal* (1971), *A Biosocial Study of the People of Bangladesh* (1973), *Population and Development Plans* (1976), *Marriage and Population Policy in India* (1979), *The Calcutta Couples: A Biosocial Profile* (1980) and *The Mentally Handicapped Children of Eastern India: A Biosocial Study* (1981). With single or joint authorship Prof. Pakrasi had substantial publications both in reputed journals in India and abroad. For example, K.B. Pakrasi., P. Dasgupta, I. Dasgupta, and P.P. Mazumder (1988) *Growth in height, weight and skinfold thickness of the Bengalee boys of Calcutta*, published in *Anthropologischer Anzeiger*, 46 : 1-18. The difficulty in the procurement of research publications of Prof. Pakrasi is a great barrier to the critical evaluation of his important contributions to the field of Anthropology.

Prof. Pakrasi served as permanent Head of the Anthropometry and Human Genetics Unit of the Indian Statistical Institute, Calcutta till his death. Unfortunately, while in service, and working in the office, he suddenly suffered a massive heart attack and died on 12th September 1987. His wife and son survive. His colleagues at the Institute had love and respect for him. His only son is a Chair Professor of Biology at

Washington University, St. Louis, U.S.A. He was a peace-loving man and a loving member of the family.

Prof. Pakrasi will be remembered by Indian anthropologists for his research contribution to anthropology.

Some important research publications

1962 Body weight at birth and incidence of low weight babies in Calcutta, India, *Anthropologie*, 23,1:81-94.

1962 A study on some aspects of the types of households and family organisation in rural Bengal, 1946-1947. *The Eastern Anthropologist*, 15,3: 55-63.

1969 Marriage and fertility among the Santal, *Bulletin of the Cultural Research Institute*, pp. 26-31.

1971 *The Uprooted: A Sociological Study of the Refugees of West Bengal*, Editions India, Calcutta.

1980 *Calcutta Couples: A Bio-social Profile*, Editions India, Calcutta.

Acknowledgement

The author thankfully acknowledges Prof. Himadri Bhusan Pakrasi, George William, and Irene Koechig Freiberg Professor, Department of Biology, Washington University, St. Louis, USA, for providing valuable information about his father Late Professor K. B. Pakrasi. The author is also indebted to Dr A. B. Das Chaudhuri, Former U.G.C. Emeritus Fellow and Professor (Retired) of the Anthropology Department, University of Calcutta for his help in writing this biography.

Chapter - 5

Indian Anthropology: The Legacy of Professor N. Subba Reddy

M.P. Damodaran

Introduction

Anthropology is an amazing discipline that strives to understand humanity. The historical development of the subject could have many shreds of evidence and instances of ups and downs, turns and twists but, overall testify how a 'speculative anthropology' or, 'arm-chair anthropology' undergoes transformation, expansion, and devises soon into an independent discipline over some time. Anthropology is hardly heard beyond the academic domain and was taught as a tiny university subject only in a few countries across the globe, till a century ago. It was also regarded as 'a kind of sacred esoteric knowledge' of certain elite upper-class people then. There was a prominence for armchair-anthropological imaginations which have been tailored predominantly to 'speculative images' of 'the others' around the world. Moreover, our discipline was 'wrongly branded', and propagated experts of the so-called tribes, primitives, natives, and so on (Damodaran, 2021:92). These are not true but, partially true since, the disciplinary horizon of anthropology has expanded 'far and wide' with a 'human-friendly perspective' by moving on its exceptional approaches, 'cultural relativism', and 'holism' (Damodaran, 2021:93,94). Interestingly, anthropology is often used by people, especially orators, speakers, scholars, researchers, politicians, and academicians to a great extent to realize its significance and subject matter. This is not only due to the recognition and appreciation of anthropology as an 'exceptional discipline', but also knowing its strength and potential (Damodaran, 2021:92).

Indian anthropology is generally considered too young, however, acknowledging it is 'the study of society and culture in India' (Beteille, 1996). It has been recognised by academic and non-academic bodies, and institutions for many decades (Sarana and Sinha, 1976:209). Distinguished anthropologists abroad, and natives of India made efforts to understand India, India's culture, and her people. During the period of British imperial administration in India, impelled and cemented anthropology by utilising it to understand the manners, and customs of the people of India. Apart from anthropologists, researchers, etc., British administrators also collected information on Indian communities and published their write-ups. Sarana and Sinha (1976:210) asserted that, 'In our view, the origin of anthropology in India goes back to the days of British colonial administration in the latter half of the nineteenth century' and Vidyarthi (2003:3) also had a similar opinion that, 'Anthropology in India originated under the influence of and to serve the purpose of the colonial administration of the British'. The journey of anthropology as one of the University Academic Disciplines only begins in the early years of the 20th century. The year, 1920 was very momentous for Indian anthropology because the teaching of anthropology was started at the University of Calcutta in this year. The University of Madras started the Department of Anthropology in a year, 1945 which was followed by a few other Universities, The University of Delhi (1948), Lucknow (1950), and Gauhati (1948, PG teaching in 1957) also opened their anthropology departments. Eventually, remarkable contributions were made by several Indian anthropologists and prompted the growth of Indian Anthropology. Thinking about the growth and progression of the discipline, a few names are coming to my mind including Professor N.Subba Reddy (1926-2018).

Remembering Professor N. Subba Reddy

I have memories of a couple of meetings with Professor N. Subba Reddy during the period, 2005-2009. First, I met him at the premises of the University of Madras in 2006 when he came to Chennai to deliver the Departmental Endowment Lectures. He held a brief chat with me and asked about my academic background and areas of research interest. In 2009, I had another opportunity to meet him at the University of Hyderabad, when I was attending the prestigious 'Indian Anthropology Congress' hosted by the Department of Anthropology, University of Hyderabad, for the National Confederation and Academy of Anthropologists (INCAA), Kolkata. Professor P. Govinda Reddy, the first Ph.D. research student, recalls that Dr Subba Reddy expects his research scholars to write their thesis by themselves with his guidance. That is why they wrote their thesis with minimum corrections to their guide. He encouraged them to come up on their own. After he retired from the University of Madras, he resided in Hyderabad with his wife Mrs. Satyavathy, and two sons, Nagarjun and Gautam.

Contribution to anthropology

Professor N. Subba Reddy (b 1926) is a distinguished scholar who tremendously contributed to the growth of Indian Anthropology for about seven decades. Professor Reddy completed his Master's Degree in 1948, and took his Doctorate in 1952 from Lucknow University, under the guidance of renowned Indian Anthropologist Professor D.N. Majumdar. A product of Lucknow University and a student of Professor Majumdar, he associated with the Ethnographic and Folk Cultural Society and the journal Eastern Anthropologist. He took up his first job as a Research Associate of a project carried out under the partnership of Cornell-Lucknow University during 1954-55. Later on, he joined the post of the Deputy Director of Kanpur Social Survey, a project of the Planning Commission, under the Directorship of Professor Majumdar. This project report of theirs was published as a book titled, '*Social Contours of an Industrial City*', in the year 1960 and was considered one of the earliest contributions to '*Urban Anthropology*' in India. The book was reprinted again in the US in the year 1975 due to its academic significance. After the completion of this project, Professor Reddy took up the post of a Lecturer at Lucknow University in the year 1956, and afterward shifted to Gauhati University, as a Lecturer in 1957, where he served as in charge of the Centre for Tribal Research and continued to hold the post till 1960. Professor Reddy started the Department of Anthropology at Andhra University. He continued to work as Head of the Department at Andhra

University from 1960, and till 1976. After he joined the University of Madras a full-fledged Department of Anthropology came into being function in 1976 with M.A., M.Phil. and Ph.D. courses.

Dr Reddy was the first Professor of Anthropology to be appointed to the Department of Anthropology, University of Madras, and also headed the Department for a decade. Professor Reddy is known for his initiatives during his tenure at Madras University, he played a crucial role in establishing the Departments of Anthropology in various Universities such as Sri Venkateswara University at Tirupati, Calicut University, Tamil University, and Hyderabad University. During his stay at Madras, he started a research journal, *South Asian Social Scientist*. He was appointed by the Tamil Nadu State Government as Chairman of the Backward Classes Commission from 1984 through 1985. He was closely associated with the Madras Institute of Development Studies and was a regular contributor to its bulletin *Madras Development Seminar Series* and its journal *Review of Development and Change*. Professor Reddy was chosen by the UGC to deliver National Lectures in 1984-85. He was a Visiting Fellow at the University of Illinois, USA, for a semester. After his retirement in 1986 from Madras University, he moved to Hyderabad and was invited as a Senior Fellow by an ICSSR institution, the Centre for Social and Economic Studies at Hyderabad during the period 1986-1991, and continued as an Honorary Professor later in the same institution. The last major project in the institution carried out was the study of 'the displacement of tribals caused by the contentious Polavaram Project' in the then Andhra Pradesh State.

Professor Reddy had a wide range of scholarship and interests. He was interested in science, scientific research, and scientific methods which were reflected in his works, literature, etc. He criticized fanciful theories, imaginary claims, and research. His writings expressed his ideas, and disciplinary stands such as social harmony, social justice, plurality, and inclusiveness. He had his credits a large number of writings and publications, which all portray his profuse interest in varied areas like Epistemology and Ethnography, Kinship, Tribal studies, Tribal development, Tribal and Naxalite movements, Dalit conflict, Caste dynamics, Village studies, Artisan castes, Farm productivity, Folklore, Displacement and Rehabilitation, Land alienation, Secularisation, Globalisation, Post-Modernism, and so on. His papers appeared in journals such as, *Contribution to Indian Sociology*, *Human Organisation*, *Economic and Political Weekly* and *Eastern Anthropologist* were momentous and showed his scholarship. The book published by the Academic Foundation, New Delhi, *Cultural Diversity and Common Humanity* (2014) included many of his vintage publications and later works. Professor Reddy also wrote several book reviews for many journals like *Eastern Anthropologist*. We could see his publications are a remarkable contribution to Indian Anthropology. Despite these, Dr Reddy, a gifted orator delivered amazing speeches, lectures, etc. He received many awards such as the *Bonnarjee Research Prize* (1954) from Lucknow University for his doctoral thesis; *Dr D.N.Majumdar Memorial Medal* (1998) from the Indian Social Science Association for his meritorious research in Social Anthropology; and *R.P. Chanda Centenary Medal* (2018) from the Asiatic Society, Kolkata for his important contribution to Anthropology. It is also worth mentioning here he was instrumental in shaping a generation of researchers and teachers. He worked hard for anthropology, its spread, and growth, in a unique manner. Professor N. Subba Reddy, the eminent Indian Anthropologist, who hails from South India, passed away on 18th December 2018, gifting us his great legacy, and unsurpassed contributions.

References

Beteille, Andre. 1996. *Caste, Class, and Power: Changing Patterns of Stratification in a Tanjore Village*. Oxford University Press, Delhi.

Damodaran, MP. 2021. You must learn anthropology! *Journal of Human Sciences*, 1, 1: 92-104.

Sarana, Gopala and Sinha Dharni P. 1976. Status of social-cultural anthropology in India, *Annual Review of Anthropology*, 5: 209-225.

Vidyarthi, LP. 2003. *Applied Anthropology in India*. Kitab Mahal, Allahabad.

Chapter - 6

Prof. S.C. Tiwari

Anup Kumar Kapoor

Prof. S.C.Tiwari's name was used everywhere in University administration, class timetables, conferences, seminars, research papers, edited books/volumes, nameplates, and many more and also, he was addressed by this name by his friends, colleagues, and teachers as well as at global and national levels. His full name was Prof. Surendra Chandra Tiwari and was born into a Brahmin family on January 24th, 1928 in proper Almora, then Uttar Pradesh (now Uttarakhand). He did his schooling from proper Almora and graduated from Allahabad University, Uttar Pradesh. After graduation, his family shifted to Delhi and he was admitted to M.Sc Anthropology, at the University of Delhi in 1948. The Department of Anthropology, University of Delhi was founded in 1947 under the Faculty of Science with Prof. P.C. Biswas as its Head when Sir Maurice Gwyer was the Vice Chancellor of Delhi University. The Department started in two rooms in the old building of the Department of Zoology, then shifted to the new building of the Arts Faculty in 1949, and later shifted to the present building in 1966. After passing his M.Sc in Anthropology in 1950, Prof. Tiwari joined the Ph.D. programme under Prof. P.C. Biswas. As Anthropology started growing in that era the focus was on physical anthropology, cultural anthropology, ethnology, dermatoglyphics, blood groups, somatometry and somatoscopy, racial types, etc. The topic of his Ph.D. was '*Ethnological Studies of the Rajis*'. The Ph.D. was awarded to him in 1959 by the University of Delhi.

It is to be mentioned here that his friend-cum-class fellow Prof. J.D. Mehra also went to the interiors of distance Almora to conduct his fieldwork for a Ph.D. Prof. J.D. Mehra's focus was on the '*Ethnological Study of Shaukas*' for almost the same years. It is interesting to mention here that I also got a chance to study Rajis and Shaukas from 1975 – 1979 and one of my students Dr P.K. Patra now teaching at Utkal University also studied Rajis for his Ph.D. work from 1998 – 2002. The final phase of fieldwork was carried out in 2015- 2017. The three-generational works on Rajis are coming up soon. During his doctorate, Prof. Tiwari also worked as an anthropologist for the Army Statistical Organisation from 1952 to 1953. Prof. Tiwari joined the Department of Anthropology, University of Delhi as a Research Assistant and became a Lecturer in the same Department in 1954. He also became a Reader (1973-1978) as well as a Professor (1977-1978). He remained in the service of the Department till January 1993.

He was awarded the Bennington Memorial Scholarship and Social Research Foundation Scholarship of the University College, London. He received advanced training in the Laboratory of Galton, U.K., and remained there for two years. He was appointed as a Research Assistant to do research under Prof. L.S. Penrose and Prof. N.A. Barnicot was the authority in Physical Anthropology/ Medical Genetics. Prof. S.C. Tiwari got advanced training in skin colour and pigmentation, haemoglobins, haptoglobins, transferrins, blood group systems, PTC, biometry, etc. After his return from the UK, Prof. Tiwari introduced all the sub-disciplines in the Department as well as in other Departments of Anthropology in India. He also started guiding his students on various topics like biochemical and serological studies, skin reflectance, dermatoglyphics, population genetics, etc.

Delhi University administration

He served as the Head of the Department of Anthropology, University of Delhi from 1984 to 1987. During this time, he was also the Dean of the Faculty of Science, Chairman of the Board of Research Studies, member of the Academic Council and Executive Council, Chairman of Open Learning School, Delhi University, Chairman of Delhi University Library System, Chairman of Governing Bodies of four different colleges.

Some of the National/ International Seminars/ Conferences organised and participated in:

- Local Secretary; *X^{th} International Congress of Anthropological and Ethnological Science,* 10 – 16 December 1978, New Delhi.
- Mentor, *International Symposium on Dermatoglyphics*, Patiala, February 1980.
- Resource Person, Indian Statistical Institute Golden Jubilee International Conference on *Human Genetics and Adaptation*, Calcutta, 1982.
- Chairman, UGC Workshop on *Modernisation of Research and Teaching in Anthropology*, February 18 – 22nd, 1983.
- Chairman, UGC National Seminar on *Perspective in Anthropological Research in India: Planning for the Future Research and Methodologies*, September 27th – October 10th, 1985.
- General Secretary, 73rd Session of Indian Science Congress Association, January 3rd – 7th, 1986.
- Chairperson, International Symposium on the *Primate: New Revolution,* December 28th– 31st, 1986.

He attended many National and International Seminars, Workshops, and Conferences.

Prof. Tiwari received research grants from various Institutions including the Ministry of Scientific Research and Cultural Affairs, Government of India; Wenner – Gren Foundation for Anthropological Research; Ministry of Environment, Government of India; ICMR, UGC, and ICSSR. He was invited to deliver the K.S. Mathur Memorial Lecture in 1985 at Lucknow University. He had been to various Universities in India and abroad assisting Professors. He used to take special classes at the Institute of Archaeology, New Delhi. He had served as President, Vice President, Chief Editor, Review Editor, etc. of many anthropological bodies like the Indian Anthropological Association, New Delhi; Ethnographic and Folk Culture Society, Lucknow; Anthropological Society of North East India, Guwahati; Indian Science Congress Association, Calcutta; Indian Anthropologist, Eastern Anthropologist, Indian Journal of Physical Anthropology and Human Genetics. He was an expert mentor for Curriculum Development in UGC; Madhya Pradesh *Uchha Shiksha Ayog*, Bhopal;

Sagar University, Madhya Pradesh; Tirupathi University, Gauhati University for Anthropology and Sociology, he has served as a capacity Professor in UGC, ICSSR, UPSC, PCS, and ICMR Prof. S.C. Tiwari got a Lifetime Achievement award in 2017 from the University of Delhi for his work in anthropology.

Prof. S.C. Tiwari published more than 100 research papers in national and international journals like Human Biology, Annals of Human Biology, Human Science, Acta Anthropo Genetica, Morpho Z. Anthropo, Human Heredity, Indian Anthropologists, Man in India, Eastern Anthropologists, The Anthropologist, Journal of Indian Anthropological Society, High Altitude Anthropology, Human Genetics, J.J. Soc. Nippon, and many more like J. Anthro. Sciavd.

He also guided more than 20 students for their PhDs some of which are as follows and all of them occupied very high status in academics or administration:- Dr Sushma Srivastava (1967), Prof. M. K. Bhasin (1968), Prof. T. Ramachanaiah (1969), Prof. A. Kalla (1968), Prof. P.K. Chattopadhyaya (1969), Dr Pramod Kalia (1971), Dr Sarla Banjee (1978), Dr Lalit Kumar (1980), Prof. Anup K. Kapoor (1981), Dr Shakuntala (1985), Dr K. Vasantha (1985), Dr Basanti Chatterjee (1989), Dr Versha Mehra (1989), Dr Swanupa Dey (1989), Dr Pradeep Roy (1991), Dr Sophia George (1994), Dr Kumud Malhotra (1992), etc

Interaction with other anthropologists in India

I observed during my 23 years with him as a student and anthropologist that any anthropologist from India who used to come to Delhi for any academic or social work would come to meet him in the Department of Anthropology, University of Delhi. I still remember when Prof. B.M. Das, Guwahati University used to come, he always brought a box of cigars for Prof. S.C. Tiwari. Prof. S.C. Tiwari was very fond of smoking cigars and perfumes. The smell of cigars through the corridors used to send the message that Prof. B.M. Das has come to the Department.

Some of the following anthropologists were very good friends as well as they had cordial interactions with Prof. S.C. Tiwari like Prof. L.P. Vidyarthi, Prof. S.C. Dube, Prof. B.M. Das, Prof. S.C.Bhagabati,

Prof. S.R.K. Chopra, Prof. J.C. Sharma, Prof. K.C. Malhotra, Prof. Usha Deka, Prof. D.P. Mukherjee, Prof. B.K. Roy Burman, Prof. K.S. Mathur, Prof. B.R. K. Shukla, Prof. P.K. Bhowmik, Prof. A. Basu, Prof. Renuka Das, Prof. L.S. Sidhu, Prof. I.J.S. Bansal, Prof. C.S. Singhrot, Prof. V. Bhalla, Prof. V.P. Chopra (Germany), Prof. J.D. Mavalwala (Canada), Prof. V. Rami Reddy, Prof.. R.N. Vashishta, Prof. B.G. Banerjee, Prof. Shalina Mehta, Prof. Banveer Singh, Prof. A Pappa Rao, as well as departmental colleagues. It is to be mentioned here that Dr B.S. Guha was his Ph.D. examiner.

Interaction as a BSc; MSc student and research scholar

I joined the Department of Anthropology, University of Delhi in 1970 as a BSc first-year student. As we had passed from a government school, we did not know the culture of wish to the teachers. We learned and always wished him and he would always respond to the student's wishes. He used to teach B.Sc second and third years about racial migration ethnology, human genetics, serological traits, material, culture and technology, and many more subdisciplines of Anthropology. At the MSc level he used to teach human population genetics, serology biochemical genetics, dermatoglyphics, and ethnology of India, as well as practical in the above subjects and craniometry osteology, and osteometry colour blindness and skin colour reflectance.

I joined his major UGC research project in September 1975 as a Junior Research Fellow and Prof. J.S. Bhandari was the Co-Principal Investigator. in the project. We left for District Pithhoragarh on 2nd October 1975 and reached Munsiari the last village in India - the Tibetan border where Bhotias as well as Rajis, Herkotiyas (Shaukas), Barbityas, and allied ethnic groups live. This first time I was exposed to the rural and tribal, low, middle, and high-altitude areas for anthropological fieldwork. I was told this is your future. Be honest, do hard work, be loyal, be patient, and many more things. I followed their advice and during my professional career occupied many administrative positions as per their positive advice.

When Prof. Tiwari visited us in the field area we went to Gangotri, Gomukh, Badrinath, Hemkunt Sahib, and many more religious places and temples in Kumaon and Garhwal Himalayas. Joshimaths and

Chamoli were also the places of our visit. He was a very religious person as he belonged to the Brahmin family.

He was always helpful to the students in class, fieldwork, and especially practical where he used to go to every student to solve his/ her problems.

He used to take special classes at the Institute of Archaeology, Government of India on craniometry (direct and indirect methods), osteology, osteometry, somatometry, somatoscopy, ageing and sexing of skull and pelvis, etc. He took classes for more than ten years at the Institute. He was accompanied by Prof. P. K. Seth, Prof. D. K. Bhattacharya, Prof. J. S. Bhandari, Prof. S. Seth, Prof. Satwanti Kapoor, and myself. The students from 1972 to 1993 in the Department always talked about his well-dressed approach, perfumed man, cigar preferences, soft spoken with manners.

About family

Prof. Tiwari used to live in a joint family. He had two brothers who were very high in positions in Govt of India. He was unmarried. He has been left with one nephew and two nieces who are IAS officers.

There are many interesting incidents about him during the field works of B.Sc and M.Sc., fieldwork in different years, and every student of that batch loved Prof. S C Tiwari because of his help, cooperation, positivity, guidance, understanding, and academic help in the field areas. He always went to the field areas with his students at B.Sc., M.Sc., and Ph.D. and guided them therein.

I still remember when there was no electricity at night (in 1984) he put anti-Rh sera in the test tube and held the tubes with the stomach of one of his fellow researchers and covered them with a blanket so that the temperature could become that and reaction could be seen.

We lost Prof. S C Tiwari on November 13th, 2022 after a brief illness. Many students learned many things from him and his life implement his advice in anthropological work and give guidance to the next generations of anthropologists.

Chapter - 7

Life Sketch of Prof. Amulya Ratan Banerjee

Diptendu Chatterjee

Historically it was from the mid-nineteenth to mid-twentieth century that Anthropology flourished as an academic discipline in Europe and America.

In India, the development of the discipline of Anthropology can be phased into three major periods initial (1920-1950), formative (1950-2000), and final (2000 onwards), Professor Amulya Ratan Banerjee one of the pioneers of the formative period passed away in the early morning of the 18th of September, 2022 at his Calcutta residence. He was born in a remote village, Dakshingram of Birbhum district, West Bengal in 1930. He was the only son amongst his four sisters born to the late Priyanath Banerjee (father) and Basanta Kumari Devi (mother). Young Banerjee passed the matriculation examination in the first division from Dakshin Gram High School in 1946. Unfortunately, his father died in 1947 and he lost his mother in a gap of seven months in the same year. In this family crisis, Banerjee moved to his eldest sister's house in Calcutta, secured admission to Ashutosh College, and completed graduation with distinction. Thereafter he chooses to study Anthropology for his post-graduation from the University of Calcutta. Having realised his deep interest in the subject Banerjee intended to devote and continue research in Anthropology for his D.Phil (Sc) degree. Finally, Banerjee was awarded a D.Phil (Sc) degree in Anthropology (1960) under the able guidance of Dr S. S. Sarkar from the University of Calcutta. His D.Phil (Sc) thesis work involved the problem of human head hair variation. This remarkable work initiated and introduced human hair research in Anthropology in India.

In his research career, he was Post Doctoral UGC Research Fellow in 1960, and Post Doctoral Research Fellow of the National Institute of Science from 1960 to 1963. In Physical Anthropology Dr Banerjee was awarded the prestigious Alexender Von Humboldt Fellowship for doing advanced research in Physical Anthropology and Human Genetics in collaboration with Prof. Von Verschuer at the Institute for Human Genetics, University of Muenster, West Germany. He did research mainly on two areas, Human Chromosome Karyotype and Bilateral symmetry and asymmetry in Anthropometric dimensions of German Twins. The karyotype of patients with the syndrome was published as a report in a Medical Bulletin in Germany. It is interesting to note that Dr Banerjee was the first Indian anthropologist to work on human chromosome karyotyping at the beginning of the 1960s. Of course, Professor S. P. Roychaudhuri (Zoologist and Cytologist) was the first researcher to do human chromosome karyotyping in India, in the early years of the 1950s.

It is well known that the model number of the human chromosome was discovered in 1956. Prof. Roychoudhuri was a world-renowned cytologist who worked with Prof. H J Muller for many years during the First World War. Prof. Muller incidentally was the second biologist to win the Noble Prize for the discovery of an induced mutation in living organisms by X-ray.

Returning to India from abroad Dr Banerjee joined the Department of Anthropology, University of Calcutta as a Lecturer at the beginning of the 1960s and retired as Professor in the 1990s. His long years of teaching and research covered different areas of Physical Anthropology such as twin biology, human hair biology, blood group polymorphism and selection, reproductive patterns of the Bengalee women, bio-social studies in India, growth studies, and forensic anthropology. Prof. Banerjee could be signed out as the only Anthropologist who was a co-founder of the blood group genetics laboratory in the Ramakrishna Mission Seva Pratisthan Hospital, Kolkata. Prof. Banerjee had much interest in forensic anthropology and he applied it in solving many criminal cases along with forensic experts. As a result, he was well connected with the organisations of Central Forensic Laboratory and State Forensic Laboratory, Kolkata, West Bengal.

Prof. Banerjee's two scholarly articles one published in Proc. Natl, Inst. Sc (B) (1963) *On variation in the medullary structure of human head hair* and the other in Z Morph. Anthrop. (1965) *On the variation of human head hair form and modulation* brought him fame as an anthropologist in India and abroad. The other paper was published by famous scientist geneticist Prof. Kurt Stern in the Annals of Human Genetics on *The genetics of hypertrichosis of the ear rim*. This was a fundamental contribution to human genetics. In the 1960s following Mendelism, several sex linked traits were found in human females but not a single trait in the human male. This was then a big question and problem among human geneticists the world over. Prof. Stern together with his co-workers including Prof. Banerjee discovered that hypertrichosis of hair in the human ear is a sex-linked trait in men.

The period from the mid-twentieth to the twenty-first century witnessed the golden age of physical anthropology and human genetics with the path-breaking research of Dr S S Sarkar, his students Prof. A R Banerjee as also by other colleagues notably Prof. D P Mukherjee, and Prof. A B Das Chaudhuri.

Prof. Banerjee has published nearly 100 scientific papers in national and international journals of repute. He attended and contributed scientific papers to an innumerable number of seminars and symposiums in India and abroad. He has supervised 16 Ph.D.s, one D.Sc, two M.D, and one M.S dissertation project.

Prof. Banerjee was associated with the Asiatic Society, Kolkata all through his academic life. He was the founder member of the Indian Anthropological Society, Kolkata, and INCAA, West Bengal, he was the Anthropological Secretary of the Asiatic Society, Kolkata during 1882-85 and 1996-99. He was sectional President of the Anthropology of the Indian Science Congress in 1999. He was the President of the Indian Academy of Forensic Sciences. He was the recipient of several awards, he got R P Chandra Medal from the Asiatic Society, Kolkata. He has delivered the prestigious Panchanan Mitra Memorial Lecture in the Asiatic Society and the prestigious Priyabala Das Memorial Lecture at Gauhati University.

In their personal life, Dr Banerjee was married to Dr Papiya Banerjee, who was the first woman to receive a Ph.D. in the Department of Anthropology, University of Calcutta. She was born in 1934 in Brahmanberia, Khulna District of Bangladesh, then East Pakistan. She graduated from Maharaja Bir Vikram College of Tripura in 1954 and an M.Sc from the University of Calcutta in 1956. Done Ph.D. from the Department of Anthropology, University of Calcutta in 1962 under the supervision of Dr S S. Sarkar. Her area of specialisation was craniometry, cephalometry, and others. She has done a Ph.D. on more than 100 skulls collected from Contai in East Medinipur district, West Bengal and later donated to the department. She was a Postdoctoral Fellow at the National Institute of Science from 1966-68. Her path-breaking work came out in the Annals of Human Genetics and American Journal of Physical Anthropology on '*Socio-economic status birth weight*'. She joined the Department of Anthropology, University of Calcutta in 1980 as a faculty member. She was a member of different learned societies and a founder member of the Indian Anthropological Society.

Both of them were some of the closest and dearest Ph.D students of Dr S.S. Sarkar. Jointly both of them did famous biological ethnographic fieldwork with Dr S. S. Sarkar in different parts of India, and as a result, two famous books by Dr S S.Sarkar came out '*Kadars of Kerala*' and '*Aboriginal Races of India*'. both of them were well attached to Prof. N K Bose.

Prof. Banerjee was truly a religious and peace-loving man and possessed the genuine qualities of a good family member. He was very soft-spoken and very affectionate to all anthropologists. I feel very proud to be associated with both of them during my research and teaching life. His direct Ph.D. student and one of the renowned Physical anthropologists is Prof. A B Das Chaudhuri, I had contact with Dr Sushil Pal, and Dr Jaya Chowdhuru, and also have contact with his last Ph.D. scholar Dr Joyita Roy, they are all the direct Ph.D. scholars of Prof. Banerjee.

Our heartfelt homage to him as a person, and a great scholar of Anthropology.

Chapter - 8

Life and Research Contribution of Prof. Usha Deka

Sarthak Sengupta

Prof. Usha Deka was born on 16th October 1931. She hailed from an elite family and her father Late Haliram Deka was Hon'ble Chief Justice (1960-1961) of Gauhati High Court, Assam. She was the second of the fourteen siblings born to Mr. Holiram Deka and Mrs. Vidyabati Deka. Her childhood and school days were spent in Calcutta.

Prof. Deka passed her matriculation from St. Margarate School, Calcutta (1946); Intermediate (1948), and Graduation (1950) from Cotton College, Guwahati with core subjects Mathematics and Physics. She had a brilliant academic career. After graduation, Prof. Deka proceeded to Calcutta and did her Post Graduation from the University of Calcutta (1952), and was awarded the University Gold Medal as the topper, besides one more medal by the University for standing first among the women candidates of the University. Although she received training and the opportunity to enrich her knowledge from some great teachers in anthropology at Calcutta University like Prof. K. P. Chattopadhyay, Prof. T. C. Roy Choudhury, Prof. T. C. Das, Prof. D. Sen, Prof. N. K. Bose, however, she imbibed great motivation from a legendary physical anthropologist of our country - Dr Sasanka Sekhar Sarkar, who often appreciated her talent and research potential.

Her background in mathematics at the undergraduate level, later in her professional career, enabled her with the competence to delve deep into the subject of quantitative human genetics. In India, there was hardly anyone among anthropologists in those days who was comparable to her intellectual stature, particularly in the field of population genetics and bio-statistics.

After obtaining an M.Sc. degree in Anthropology, she carried out research work at the Directorate of Research, NEFA (now Arunachal Pradesh) as an Assistant Research Officer and worked there with the famous anthropologist Dr Verrier Elwin from 1952 to 1954. In 1954, she married renowned anthropologist Prof. L.K. Mahapatra. She started her teaching career as a Lecturer in the Department of Anthropology, Lucknow University (1954-1956) and later moved to Gauhati University in 1956-1964 and worked with Prof. M. C. Goswami, and Prof. B.M. Das. She was awarded an Alexander von Humboldt Senior Fellowship, West Germany (1956-1960), and earned her Doctorate in Science (Dr rer. nat.) in 1960 from the Christian Albrecht's University, Kiel, Germany under the supervision of Dr J. Schaeuble for her work on the finger and palmar dermatoglyphics of criminals (*Studies an Handabrucken Von Verbrechern Aus Deutschland*).

After her return to India from Kiel, West Germany she rejoined and remained attached to the Department of Anthropology, Gauhati University for a brief spell (till May 1964), then she moved over and joined the Department of Anthropology, Utkal University, Vani Vihar, Bhubaneswar as Reader in the year 1964 when the department was only six years old, where she served in different capacities and elevated to the post of Professor in 1985, and superannuated as a Professor of Physical Anthropology in 1991. She was an anthropologist of international repute. Prof. Deka held several distinguished positions in India including Vice President of the Indian Anthropology Association, New Delhi in 1985 and member of State Advisory Board of Orissa State Museum, Bhubaneswar; to name only a few. She was offered visiting positions at many famous Indian Universities.

Prof. Deka was an excellent and loving teacher, however, her sharp-edged tongue, strong will, and uncompromising attitude toward dishonest activities earned her many critics. She appeared to be rigid at times and harsh externally but was soft and affectionate at heart. She was a very strict disciplinarian, punctual, sincere, and honest. Her life as such was full of trials and challenges. Life has presented her with many hurdles, yet, she bore the pains of lonely life silently, circumvented all with dignity, alacrity, and talents without succumbing to them.

The research areas covered by Prof. Deka are in the fields of population genetics, demography, anthropometry, dermatoglyphics, somatic growth, and maturity (through both cross-sectional and longitudinal methods, micro-evolutionary dynamics in numerically small population groups, etc., on a wide variety of populations of Orissa, Assam, and Meghalaya and the results of the studies conducted are disseminated through publications in peer-reviewed journals, edited volumes, books, reports, lectures and proceedings of several technical seminars. Before the initiation of the research investigation by Prof. Deka, hardly any systematic genetic data were available to understand the nature of biological diversity amongst the population groups of Orissa.

To establish a vibrant population genetical laboratory at the Department of Anthropology, Utkal University, initially, Professor Deka initiated a systematic bio-anthropological investigation along with her Post Graduate students encouraging them to collect information on ABO blood groups, PTC taste sensitivity, screening of red-green colour blindness whenever they visit their countryside home during vacation which resulted in amassing data on various genetic traits on a wide variety of hitherto lesser-known population groups of Orissa.

During her tenure as a faculty member of the Department of Anthropology, at Utkal University, Prof. Usha Deka completed two major research projects with financial assistance from the University Grants Commission, New Delhi. These are:

(i) *Anthropometric Study of the Malva (Pentiya) of Koraput district, Orissa*; and;

(ii) *Anthropometric Studies of Kansaris of Orissa*.

Prof. Deka was far away from producing frivolous research writings. During her tenure at Gauhati University, she published a few research articles with Prof. B.M. Das on a least studied caste of Assam–Suri, who now identify themselves as Baishya.

To understand her area of research interest, one should be acquainted with the research work that she carried out through her research students. Her thought-provoking research article on '*Fertility and reproductive wastage*' was published in *Tribal Demography of*

India (edited by R.N. Pati and L. Jagatdeb) in 1991. One more article having a similar title (with P. Patojoshi) was also published in the *Bulletin of the Department of Anthropology, Dibrugarh University* in 1978.

Prof. Deka has mentored around ten Ph.Ds, and all these doctoral dissertations were highly praised by the academic world. Many of her students have been highly placed in reputed academic institutions. Apart from Utkal University, Vani Vihar, Prof. Deka was recognised Ph.D. Research Guide of Sambalpur and Berhampur University also.

Among her Ph.D. students, Dr. S. K. Ghosh Maulik (1977) worked on a *Demogenetic Study of a Population: The Siyalgirs*, a numerically small rural community of Orissa. Dr P. N. Sahu (1978) studied another numerically small genetic isolate in the fringe areas of Bhubaneswar, Orisha. Both the population were little over one thousand numerically, and with a very low admixture rate. The study reveals that the survival strategy of both populations is regulated by varied occupation types, social systems, and cultural practices.

Dr P.K. Patojoshi (1977) studied the *Somatic and Genetic Variation among the Gadabas of Orissa*. The study was confined to two linguistically distinct sub-groups - Mundari-speaking *Gutab* and Dravidian-speaking *Ollar*, besides one more sub-group called *Sena*. The study indicates very limited genetic variation within the *Gutab*, an example of a convergent type of micro-evolution, as they are confined to a small territory.

Dr S. Patel (1980) studied the process of adaptation of Tibetan migrants rehabilitated in the Chandragiri hills of South Orissa. How these high-altitude Tibetans adapt themselves biologically and culturally was thoroughly investigated. The study reveals that cultural adaptation is relatively quicker than biological adaptive changes which are expected to come down the generations.

Dr J. Kanungo (1982) conducted a meticulous study on the *Fertility Variation among the Oriya Castes in Urban Communities*.

Dr G. Nayak (1983) studied the *Racial Affinities of the Khonds of Orissa*. Khonds of Orissa are subdivided into three sub-groups. Her study indicates the existence of mutual segregation, however, not of a very diverse nature concerning morphological and genetic characteristics.

Prof. P. K. Das (1983) attempted to understand the nature and extent of genetic segregation and relative divergence between the Mundari-speaking tribal population of Koraput and Ganjam districts of Orissa based on language, following the linguistic classification of Norman Zide. The study supports the linguistic dendrogram of Norman Zide and confirms that language acts as a potent factor in the origin of genetic diversity.

Variation of Menarche in Oriya Women and its various correlations with socioeconomic and other relevant factors was assessed by Dr B. Patnaik (1987).

The practice of consanguinity/inbreeding in the perspective of social and cultural tradition and its impact also attracted her attention and such practices in two cities of Orissa and a traditional community of south Orissa were also thoroughly investigated.

In India, the pattern of body growth is mainly assessed through the cross-sectional method. It was Dr B. Rath (1976) who studied the growth of Oriya children through the longitudinal method. One more study on this less-trodden area was conducted by Dr S. Nanda (1993; *Study on Secular Growth Trend in Orissa*) who also ventured to conduct a growth study following a time-consuming longitudinal method among the villagers.

Prof. Deka collected a large number of prehistoric lithic implements from open sites in different parts of Orissa. Some of these lithic artifacts were later properly analyzed and reported by some of her competent colleagues.

She was elected as Recorder of the Anthropology and Archaeology Section of the Indian Science Congress Association, held at Kharagpur (1970), and in 1980, she was elected President of the Anthropology and Archaeology Section of the Indian Science Congress in its 67th Session at Jadavpur, West Bengal. She delivered an illuminating speech on the '*Taxonomic relationship among the Hindu population of Orissa*'. She was the Vice-President of the Indian Anthropology Association, New Delhi (1985).

Although Prof. Deka was away from her home state Assam for a prolonged period due to her professional obligations, she was very much concerned about the 'Assam Movement' which started during the seventies of the last century. She studied the movement in great detail and authored a small treatise '*Background of Assam Movement*' in 1981 which was co-authored by Mr. Devajyoti Deka and published by Bani Prakash, Guwahati, Assam. The book details how the discontent and sense of deprivation brewed in Assamese hearts for a long time gradually culminated in the movement. She opines that 'discontent and deprivation' are constant factors of the Assamese experience. Here, Prof. Deka speaks more like a social analyst.

It is most unfortunate that, during her professional career, Prof. Deka did not receive due recognition of her merit and innovative spirit from her peers. She was very straightforward, strict disciplinarian, courageous, and above all kindhearted.

Prof. Usha Deka is no more with us. She passed away on 17th June 2014 afternoon at the age of 83 years. With her demise, the Anthropology fraternity in India in general, and Assam, in particular, has become poorer. Her demise created a void in the field of biological anthropology in India and perhaps an era in the biological anthropology of our country has come to an end. Biological Anthropologists of India, however, owe a great deal to her.

Some of her research publications are:

(i) Fingerprint of the Suri (jointly with B.M. Das), *Journal of Gauhati University,* 9:121-126, 1958.

(ii) Physical characters of the Suri of Assam (jointly with B.M. Das), *Journal of Gauhati University,* 11,2:87-98, 1960.

(iii) Growth during adolescence among Oriya boys and girls. *Journal of Indian Anthropological Society,*4:141-146.1969.

(iv) Study of fertility in a tribe of North East India. *Journal of Social Research,*1,12:74-82.1970.

(v) PTC taste threshold in some castes of Orissa, *Adibasi,* 11,3:7-13. 1969-1970.

(vi) Palmar dermatoglyphics of the Mundas of Orissa, (jointly with P. Behera), *Man in India*, 50,2:54-59, 1970.

(vii) Fertility in some groups of Orissa. *Man in Society,* 51-62. 1972.

(viii) Earlobe variation in various populations of Assam (jointly with P.B. Das), *Man in India,*33:256-261.

(ix) Genetic survey of the Gadabas of Orissa, (jointly with P. Patojoshi), *Man In India.* 55,3. 1975.

(x) Anthropogenetic study of the Pentia Halvas of Koraput District, (jointly with S. K. Ghosh Maulik), *Adibasi,*16,3:18-36,1976.

(xi) Growth and economic condition of Oriya urban children, (jointly with B. Rath), *Bulletin of the Department of Anthropology, Dibrugarh University*, 6:181-192,1977.

(xii) Fertility and pregnancy wastage (jointly with P. Patojoshi), *Bulletin of the Department of Anthropology, Dibrugarh University*, 6:192-199, 1977.

(xiii) *Background of Assam Movement* (jointly with Mr. Devajyoti Deka), Bani Prakash, Guwahati, Assam, 1981.

(xiv) Fertility and reproductive wastage, in R.N. Pati and L Jagatdeb (Eds): *Tribal Demography of India*, Ashish Publication House, New Delhi, 1991.

Acknowledgement

I am thankful and indebted to Dr Premananda Bharati, former Professor at Indian Statistical Institute, Kolkata, for his sincere academic support in preparing this write-up.

Chapter - 9

Life and Works of Dr P.R.G. Mathur

P.K. Misra

PRG as I affectionately called Dr Mathur was my colleague at the Anthropological Survey of India (AnSI) and friend for more than 60 years. It was indeed a long journey traveled together. I bow down and offer my *shradhanjli* to him.

The more I think of him after his departure more I realise that he was an outstanding person, a scholar, totally committed to research, continuously searching for new areas to work, and a humanist to the core. He covered a wide variety of subjects in his research. Rigorous fieldwork was his forte and indeed it is amazing that he went on to do fieldwork on widely different subjects. He openly condemned the practice of obtaining data through research students. His concern for the poor and downtrodden was total. He strongly believed in the application of anthropological knowledge for the welfare of the people. He was hyper-critical of the people who obtained falsely scheduled caste or tribe certificates. He was prepared to go to any extent to prove their guilt.

After his stint in AnSI., he came back to Kerala, he not only changed his dress to a white *khadi panchey* and a loose bush shirt and allowed his bear to grow. Over the years it became fully grey which gave him a saintly and senior citizen look.

In a caste-ridden society, he rose from a humble background so to say, and went on to the pinnacle of his profession. For his studies on one side, he was rubbing shoulders with Mappila fisher folk and on the other with the most sacred Brahmins of Gurvayur and Sabrimala Ayyappa temples. He handled these sensitive and contradictory roles smoothly with the sole objective of obtaining authentic and relevant data. He was never tired when it came to doing field work; I have reported elsewhere that once we were taking Fredric Barth, one of the pioneers of the research on nomads around Kerala. On the way, we noticed a group of duck rearers taking their stock across agricultural fields. He abruptly asked the Jeep driver to stop. Even before it came to a halt he jumped out of it and got hold of the leader of the group. He sat down with him on the roadside and began his interview. He not only collected some relevant data about the group but also a detailed genealogy of the person completely oblivious that we had a foreign scholar with us waiting for him to return. He came back loudly announcing to me that he had collected some valuable data on the nomadic duck keepers for my research. Barth appreciated what Mathur did but he openly confessed that he could not have done it with his subjects in South Persia.

How I came to know him

I joined AnSI in 1958, a couple of months later Prof. Nirmal Kumar Bose the then Director of AnSI launched the study of the distribution of the *Material Traits Survey* (MTS) in rural areas of India. I and Shri S.K. Ganguli did a pilot study for this project in central India. Based on our findings the study was undertaken at the all-India level for which 16 scholars were appointed to conduct the MTS. PRG Mathur was one of them. The whole operation of the project was to be conducted from the Central India Station of AnSI at Nagpur under the supervision of Dr S.C. Sinha. Since two of us (I and Ganguli) had conducted the pilot survey we were asked to explain the project to the new scholars who joined the team and train them to collect data by taking them to a village. That is how I came to know of PRG Mathur. The memories of that period have faded not only owing to a long time gap but also because we were all concerned about our next field destinations in a time-bound project. Our immediate boss Surajit Sinha was always friendly, sympathetic, and understanding but when it came to the schedule of the MTS there was no compromise as his *Guru* and director of the project Professor Nirmal Kumar Bose a Gandhian, a self-disciplined person expected the same from all those who worked with him. At that time we did not have much time to interact with him. Later when each one of us returned from our respective fields and got assembled at Kolkata we began to know each other and exchange our field data for finalisation of the report. Once that was done we got busy with our next research assignments. The next research assignments were part of a great design that Professor Bose had in mind. Let me digress a little because this phase proved to be a watershed in the research careers of some of us who worked in MTS which includes scholars like Mathur, B.N. Saraswati, N.K. Behura, Bikas Rai Chouduri, S.G. Morab, and Rajalakshmi to name only a few.

Bose was a Gandhian in thought but in practice, he appeared benignly aggressive and certainly a person in a hurry. Bose was fiercely independent. He could differ from Gandhi and let him know about it. Bose was, 'driven by the indomitable spirit of inquiry: he transgressed the boundaries of specific disciplines and the conventional divides between theoretical thinking and application of knowledge' (Sinha, 1984:1). He was perhaps the only nationalist anthropologist India has known. The field of anthropology is as well-known has been dominated by colonial concerns. The Indian anthropologists did little to change those concerns. Bose felt rather strongly that they simply followed what was prevalent in the West. He expressed such views in several of his writings (Bose, 1952:56, 1963:1). He wanted to chart out a course that reflected Indian reality and knowledge. He wanted the perspective of India as a whole should be kept in view while studying at different levels of material, organisational, and abstract and also interconnection between them. He was concerned to demonstrate the characteristic features of Indian civilisation and show its underlying unity. He forcefully argued, 'there is more unity in India's variety than is likely to admit in moments of forgetfulness' (1961: VII). He visualised that the structure of Indian society was like a pyramid. There was more differentiation at the material base of life and progressively less at the social organisational level and further at the level of ideas and philosophy. He wanted anthropological research should reflect the reality of India so that the basic task of regenerating the colonially subjugated nation could be taken up scientifically. No sooner did he get an opportunity in 1959 when he became director of the Anthropological Survey of India (AnSI) he initiated research projects of AnSI towards that end. MTS was the first research activity among them. He had two very important objectives in undertaking this project. The first was to generate data on material traits at all India levels and the second was to rigorously train young scholars he had recruited for systematic observation and record. He was very particular about it. Bose, unfolded his grand plan for research in the AnSI after the successful completion of MTS, which has been systematically outlined by Sinha (1973:8). That is how the study of pottery, metal crafts, the social organisation of ancient crafts, fisherfolks, nomads, temples, and centers of religious learning followed. In other words, the contours of the Indian civilisation were being approached from different vantage points. This way Bose and Sinha had built a team of research workers who took his idea forward. After completion of MTS Mathur opted to study fisherfolk Mappila in Kerala and I went to Rajasthan to study the nomadic Gadulia Lohars. So again we lost active contact with each other. These studies took several years to complete. But finally, I settled down in Mysore and he in Kozhikode when our contacts not only became more regular but we intensively interacted on various issues of anthropological interests. Before I discuss selections from his major anthropological contributions let me quickly give a brief sketch of his bio-data.

Bio-data

He was born in Mathur village, Palakkad district, Kerala. His primary education was done in the village school, for his secondary and higher education he went to Palakkad. He acquired his Master's Degree in Sociology and Anthropology from Agra University, Agra. He earned a Ph.D. from Calcutta University, in 1973. His Ph.D. thesis was on the Mappila fisher folk of Kerala which was guided by Professor Surajit Sinha. He served AnSI for 15 years from 1959 to 1973. In 1973, he returned to Kerala as a Special Officer of the Tribal Research and Training Centre, Government of Kerala, Calicut which was hitherto held by the celebrated anthropologist, Professor A. Aiyappan. This institute was upgraded and renamed as Kerala Institute for Research, Training and Development Studies of Scheduled Castes and Scheduled Tribes (KIRTADS) of which he became the first director. Under his stewardship from 1979 to 1987, this institute conducted a variety of studies on scheduled communities and also conducted numerous seminars, conferences, and workshops, and also organised many training programmes for the officers of the state government engaged in the welfare of scheduled communities. He became the Director and Professor of Ananthakrishna Iyer International Centre for Anthropological Studies, Mathur Agraharam, Palakkad, Kerala. He was the Chairman of the International Commission on Urgent Anthropological Research, South Indian Regional Centre, Palakkad. He founded Muddha Moopan Centre for Tribal Medicine Development Hospital at Mathur of which he was the Managing Trustee. He was passionately involved in patronizing this center which also is a testimony of his commitment to the application of anthropological knowledge for the welfare of the people as well as his passion for the promotion of traditional practices.

Major contributions

Mathur's anthropological professional career spanned approximately six decades. He was a devoted researcher himself and after he became the director of the Tribal Research Institute, he guided the research of many scholars. His research interest was, spread over a variety of subjects but from his voluminous bibliography, it could be said that the study of tribes, fishing communities, sacred complexes, development, and application of anthropological knowledge were the main ones. But his other contributions such as *Caste Councils among the Namputiri Brahmins of Kerala*, in The Eastern Anthropologist, Vol. XXII, No. 2, 1969: *Caste Councils among the Ezhavas of Kerala* in Proceedings of World Malayalam Conference, 1975; *Tribal Medicine: A Study of Irular Science and Superstition*, in Tribal Thought and Culture in honour of Surajit Sinha, edited by B.N. Saraswati; *Customary Law among the Matrilineal Tribes* in Encyclopaedia of Dravidian Tribes Vol.1 pp. 305-313 edited by T. Madhav Menon, 1996; *Devadasis of Kerala* in Studies in Indian Anthropology, edited by P.K. Misra, Rawat Publication, 2004; *Sanskritisation of Non-Brahman Communities in Kerala* in M.N. Srinivas: the Man and His Work, edited by P.K. Misra et al., Rawat Publication, 2007 were landmark publications. Whatever subject he chose he dealt with it in depth. However, here I will concentrate on three areas, namely his study of fisherfolks, studies of tribes, and study of the sacred complex. The reason I have selected them; his first major intensive field investigation started with the study of the Mappila, the study of tribes remained his lifelong interest and official obligation because he became the director of the tribal research institute in Kerala, then in his later phase of life his spiritual devotion coaxed him to apply his anthropological understanding in discovering various aspects of sacred complexes. In this respect study of sacred complexes was truly done in a participant observer manner.

Study of fisherfolks

Marine fisherfolks operate in two distinct ecological regions: the sea and the land. While the sea provides them resources for their existence land provides them the opportunity to interact with other human beings, exchange their goods, and obtain certain services required for their day-to-day living as well as for celebrating life cycle rituals and festivals. To extract resources from the sea the fisherfolks have to develop an understanding of the ways of the sea, which is, what they see as facts, what they imagine, and what is handed down to them as part of their traditions. For all this, they have to systematically observe its waters, currents, waves, winds, fauna, flora, and the cosmos that envelops it all. They have to classify and codify all such information according to their understanding and values. This has to be underlined that in the case of the marine fisher folks, all such knowledge is of critical importance for them not only for their subsistence but also for their survival. Any venture into the sea is potentially risky and is full of suspense and therefore it has to be correct. All relevant parameters have to be properly noted, read, and correctly deciphered for a successful, productive, and safe trip. The sea is immense and much of it hitherto has remained 'beyond' both in-depth and expanse to the members of any fishing community. For the same reason, the sea is associated with awe and mystery. Its tremendous power and potentialities, its unpredictable behaviour, etc., have to be in the perception of the fisher folks in their day-to-day decision-making process. Thus, marine fisher folks are a unique set of people. India has a huge coastline and expectedly marine fishing has been the primary means of livelihood for a large section of the population of India since prehistoric times yet the anthropologists have virtually neglected their study. The AnSI in 1967 decided to fill in this gap and accordingly, Mathur who was then working in it decided to work on the Mappila fisherfolk of Kerala under the guidance of Dr Surajit Chandra Sinha, former Vice Chancellor of Visva-Bharati. He conducted an intensive field investigation in a village inhabited by the Mappila fisherfolk in the Malappuram district of Kerala. He made two field trips and spent about nine months with them. He also visited some neighbouring villages. Based on this fieldwork, he produced a book entitled *The Mappila Fisherfolk of Kerala* (1977) published by the Kerala Historical Society, Trivandrum. It is a pioneering work and extremely rich in providing ethnographic details. He has shown that the fishing economy of the Mappila is inseparable from their kinship structure, rituals, and belief systems. Mathur provides a wealth of information on Mappila's knowledge of the marine environment and cosmology. It is worthwhile to mention that Mappila identifies eleven types of waves, eight kinds of winds, and eight kinds of currents. They carefully mobilise their knowledge and technical resources in trapping different kinds of fish. Mathur's work convinces us that though Mappila may be illiterate in the modern sense of the term make rational choices based on their empirical knowledge of the marine environment. The Mappila fisherfolk are Muslims and are divided into distinct endogamous caste-like groups graded in a status hierarchy. The book is well illustrated with relevant sketches and photographs and would remain basic in marine fishing. This is important to note that in the last few decades, significant changes have taken place in the technology of fishing, transportation of the yields, and several other fields and therefore what Mathur has produced provides authentic baseline data for those interested in change.

Mathur produced another book on fishing entitled *Ecology, Technology, and Economy* (2008) jointly published by Indira Gandhi Rashtriya Manav Sangrahalaya, Bhopal and Rawat Publications, Jaipur. After doing fieldwork among the Mappila 1970-72, Dr PRG Mathur did some fieldwork among some Hindu fisherfolk in 1980-82 and then again he did fieldwork in 2006 among some other fishing communities which is the basis of his second book on fisherfolk. Both in terms of time, depth and spatial spread of his studies, he was in a unique position to provide insight as to what is happening to the fisher folk in Kerala.

In the second book, his objective was to cover a maximum number of fishing communities in Kerala and provide ethnographic details about them, and also the kind of adaptation they were making under the changed circumstances. His previous studies on fisherfolk provide a rich and substantial background and experience for undertaking his later studies. To cover a maximum number of fishing communities in the shortest possible time for these studies he made some significant methodological innovations. For example, he demarcated three major regions of fisherfolk in Kerala. From each region, he selected 3 to 5 fishing communities. The idea was to capture significant variations among the communities concerning their fishing operations, their traditional knowledge, trade, rituals, and development.

No doubt there have been many changes since Mathur did his first fieldwork among the fisherfolk of which the introduction of sophisticated technology in fishing operations was the most significant. These innovations so to say have reduced the limitations imposed by nature. Now trawlers can sweep the ocean clean of any object moving or crawling. Echo sounders or fish finders can pick up even the weakest signals generated by fish even at the bottom of the ocean. GPS and constant weather monitoring systems have certainly considerably reduced the hazards of marine fishing. These along with rapid changes in communication, transport, and refrigeration facilities have not only enormously increased the yield, but also expanded the market and profitability of the enterprise. All these certainly have generated enormous wealth and power at least for a few and a lot of opportunities for fishermen in general. Interestingly all these profound changes did not prompt large-scale economic diversification. Maybe marine fishing still has tremendous potential though serious concerns about the regeneration of resources have arisen which led authorities to impose certain restrictions on fishing and the use of certain technology during certain seasons. The long-term ecological impact of the new technologies, intense competition, and effort to maximize profit are going to be very serious and also on the communities and people who cannot afford the astronomical cost of modern technology. Mathur has shown the role of banks and middlemen has increased enormously as a result of that stranglehold on weaker sections and real workers have become tighter. One may rightly ask where the level playing field is for them; the world is becoming flatter or pyramidal. However, it is interesting to note that fisher folk society and culture have shown remarkable resilience. The caste and community identities have remained intact along with respective cultural, and ritual practices and values associated with status and hierarchy. Gender discrimination too continues. It is legitimate to point out that the existence of them along with revolutionary changes in technology and globalisation are intriguing, particularly in the context of Kerala which is considered to be a model state from a development perspective. His studies once again point out that the caste question in India in general and in Kerala, in particular, are extremely complex. The jostling among those who are in the caste system and even with those who had gone out of the Hindu society for higher status is interesting. This jostling continues to make the concept of 'purity' relevant as well as the path that they take to raise the status in the caste hierarchy though there have been some new interpretations of symbols they adopt. The detailed observations of Mathur in his later studies and the one on Mappila, along with that of Arne Martin Klausen (1968) a Norwegian are extremely useful and relevant for developing meaningful discourse on change, particularly in the wake of profound technological and political changes in the wider arena. It may be mentioned that Klausen in his study focussed on the classical question as to why there was unequal response by different communities to the development stimuli.

Study of tribe

Mathur has published a large number of articles on tribes in different journals and occasional publications. Besides a book on a tribe in Odisha and a book on the Khasi of Meghalaya, a bulk of his writings on tribes are in Kerala and that too which is located in the Wynaad region. His book *Tribal Situation in Kerala* (1977) is a collection of his essays and was published by the Kerala Historical Society. The articles included in this volume were written between 1973-76 in response to a specific invitation for some seminar or workshop for his contribution. Dr K.S. Singh, former director of the Anthropological Survey of India in his foreword of the book writes that in 1969 the Indian Institute of Advanced Study, Shimla convened a seminar on tribal situation in India which stimulated efforts in many parts of the country to build up regional profiles of tribal situation. Mathur's book is one such effort in that direction. He further writes 'Ultimately, regional studies like this that will help build up a truly national and all India picture of a tribal picture of tribal situations with a rich pattern of regional diversities and variations' (1977: IX).

The book begins with the Introduction: Tribal Demography: An Appraisal. In this chapter, after giving a demographic picture of the tribes in India he focuses on tribes in Kerala. He identifies seven tribal regions in Kerala and describes a characteristic feature of tribes in each region. While summing up he makes an important observation that the tribal communities not only differ from one another but also from their neighbouring non-tribals. He observes that 'two tribes speaking different dialects belonging to the same linguistic family may sometimes vary in their means of subsistence whereas there may be two tribes of more or less the same economic pursuits, who have no linguistic affinities' (ibid:9). This observation, in particular, should be noted by the scholars who build pictures of the migration of populations in a hurry. Besides the introduction, the book is divided into four parts namely, I. Primitive Tribal Communities, II. Tribal Situation: Perspective and Problems, III. Tribal Development and Integration and IV. Movements and Leadership. The tribes he has described under Primitive Tribal Communities (hereafter Particularly Vulnerable Tribal Groups, acronym PVTGs) are Cholanaikan and Kurumbas of Attapady. Under the Tribal Situation, he has described the transfer and alienation of tribal land and bonded labour system and the perpetual indebtedness of the tribes in Attapady. The strength of his description lies in the fact that he has given the details of the cases of indebtedness and how year after year the so-called contract of bondage is renewed in front of a deity. The chapter that follows is focused on the issue of electrification in tribal areas. He notes that the use of electricity in the tribal area particularly in Wynaad is minimal. He wryly writes 'all the tribal houses except an M. L. A. and three Mullu Kurumbas are reported to be without electricity' (ibid; 131). The following chapters focus on the government residential school in Wynaad and the status of women in some of the tribes in Kerala. It is important to note that there are significant differences among the selected tribes. The last part is focused on the tribal movement in Wynaad. In this chapter, Mathur has briefly discussed that most of the forest areas in the Wynaad in the past were under feudal control during which time 'extensive tracts of tribal land have been surreptitiously acquired or usurped by who are immigrants from the plains, particularly from Travancore area' (ibid: 187). After independence and liquidation of feudal control, there was an intense influx of people from outside the region which led to further dispossession of tribes from the base of their life-support resources. Over time, several political parties became active. Mathur briefly touches on the Naxal movement which in Kerala started from Wynaad.

The strength of this book lies in that he has scrupulously followed the anthropological dictum of describing the facts as seen by him and highlighting the problems of the tribes in the region. Since Mathur has been very much concerned about the development of the tribes at the end of each chapter he has given his suggestions too. One of the serious flaws is that like most anthropologists, he is carried away by the erroneous categorisation of some people as primitive and they being isolated. This is not the place to discuss this issue here but must be mentioned that the forest has been a most important resource base in Indian civilisation. The extraction of those resources has been largely in the hands of professional forest dwellers for their consumption and also for trade with the peasantry under various kinds of arrangements. These arrangements were greatly shaken owing to colonial penetration, massive extraction of timber, and the introduction of a plantation economy in forest regions. The people living in the forest were made primitive and also subject to massive and inhuman exploitation (see Misra, 2018).

Study of the Sacred Complex

Mathur produced two significant studies on the sacred complex. After his exhaustive and very well-illustrated study of Gurvayur, he wrote an equally valuable book on the Sabarimala Ayyappa temple. Sabarimala Ayyappa temple is not only anthropologically relevant it has acquired political significance too and hence I would like to discuss it in a little more detail. Also because of the time when Mathur conducted this study, he was not well. But he was determined to do the work. He despite his poor health made several trips to the temple of course since he could not climb he had to hire a palanquin to go up. Owing to his determination and sheer strong willpower he completed the work. The astonishing thing was that he did not want to miss any detail of any of the rituals that were conducted there. And from early morning to evening a large number of rituals were conducted there. All the well-wishers of Mathur and functionaries of the temple were worried about the health of Mathur. Yet in his simple yet pure ethnographic account of the temple he has produced a text which continues to draw the attention of scholars interested in religion as well as common people wanting to know an authentic account of the sacred complex associated with Sabarimala Ayyappa temple. It would be a huge understatement to state that it attracts thousands and thousands of pilgrims every year. On one hand, the curiosities of the people in trying to understand the cosmos and relate them to in their day-to-day life, and on the other the uncertainties they face in real day-to-day life are eternal issues and continue despite all modernisation and development of science. Hence places like Sabarimala will continue to be relevant for people at large seeking the grace of all mighty. In recent decades the popularity of the Sabarimala temple has exponentially grown.

Sabarimala pilgrimage center is located on a hilltop and in a forested area. The location of sacred deities in forests and on the top of hills is not an isolated phenomenon in Indian civilisation but its significance has not been fully discussed in the extant literature from the point of view of understanding the position of the forest-dwelling people in the larger Indian society and their relationship with it. Though the Sabarimala region is inhabited by several tribal groups their involvement in the ritual complex at Sabarimala is minimal. Mathur has convincingly shown that Ayyappa is associated with a hunting deity and those who are making the first pilgrimage to Sabarimala have to undergo a ritual that is reminiscent of hunting expeditions. Yet it has been incorporated as part of the great Sanskritic tradition. The learned Brahmins conduct all the proceedings and the deity is considered to be part of the Hindu pantheon. How did this happen? It indicates that there must have been a long period of interaction between folk and literati. This interaction certainly needs to be underlined to understand the making of the Indian civilisation in which folk traditions were like tributaries to the mainstream. The process through which it was achieved needs to be researched in each case.

The mythologies associated with the Ayyappa Swami are unique. It is believed that Ayyappa (Hariharaputra) is born of the union of Mohini (Vishnu) and Siva. Women devotees in the reproductive phase of their lives are prohibited from entering the temple. Even the form in which Ayyappa Swami is depicted is so very different. He is in a squatting posture and his knees are held together by a band called Yoga-patta. His face is lively with eyes open. There are eighteen sacred steps to reach the temple and are considered to be significant in performing the pilgrimage. It is important to note that the Sabarimala temple is open to all irrespective of caste, creed, or religion. Brahmins have incorporated the deity in the Hindu pantheon. They have also generated a cult around the deity and a certain procedure for the pilgrims to follow in which the community identity of the people on pilgrimage is temporarily suspended and those visiting the temple have only one identity and that is of a devotee to the deity, and accordingly, they address each other not by their names or community identity but as a devotee of Ayyappa Swami. They observe a strict code of conduct for 41 days and have an elevated sense of spirituality and equality. They offer prayers in the mornings and evenings and get into a frenzy creating an environment of spirituality and sacredness, and equally important is the fact that all differences are dissolved. This particular aspect is significant as the Hindu religion is dominated by the idea of ritual purity and pollution in almost all aspects of traditional life especially when it comes to religious practices. These and many more features associated with the temple complex certainly raise many questions and issues for understanding the role of religion in society and the making of Indian civilisation. Mathur finds that the Ayyappa cult exercises unique influence over the socio-religious and political life of South India. The cult is an amalgamation of diverse faiths like tribal religion, Brahminical religion, the Buddhist tradition, Saivism, and Tantric tradition. It even incorporates obeisance to a Muslim saint.

There is a dire need to work out an authentic and systematic political history of the region highlighting the role of religion in extending control over the frontier regions. There is a definite reason for doing so because these frontier regions were inhabited by a variety of forest-dwelling people fiercely conscious of their autonomy. Forest has always been a rich and diverse resource base and therefore has been of critical importance to the growing needs of all. The people in power would like to have control over those resources and their extractions, and also keep the frontiers secure. The denizens of the forest, in the past thus played an important role as a bridge and buffer between powerful kingdoms. Of course, this situation dramatically changed during the colonial regime. Besides, this study of Mathur indicates a spiritual link between forest dwellers and the greater Indian civilisation. In the past, these aspects had not been systematically explored as the anthropological interest grew during the colonial period in which it was taken for granted that the forest-dwelling people were isolated, were without history, and had no ability for abstraction. Mathur's study repeatedly draws attention to the presence of the folk element in the whole Ayyappa temple complex. He has a vast experience in tribal studies in India.

In this study, Mathur has done the basic work, systematically and rigorously applying anthropological techniques. He made several trips to the temple both as a scholar and as a devotee. His zeal to carry on with research and probe deeper and deeper has remained ever-green. In this study, he has done pioneering work and also has raised many serious questions which need to be further researched.

There is a whole range of legends associated with the shrine which certainly indicates its antiquity and also that so many different communities are involved in it that each has tried to interpret it according to their understanding and tradition. However, the major task ahead would be systematic interpretations of the stories, symbols, and rituals of the temple complex. However, the situation has become complex because of the promotion of religious tourism. The volume of traffic to the hills particularly on pilgrimage days has enormously grown. The management of this has become a serious problem. Commercial interest plus political posturing of different interest groups have become apparent if not more dominant. There are conflicts of interest leading courts to intervene. It is indeed a paradox as to how modern courts based on reason and rationality can resolve conflicts arising out of faith but the state has responsibilities that cannot be wished away particularly when there is such a large congregation of people. The emerging problems are real and urgent. One of which is an environmental concern. Mathur has highlighted the environmental impact of commercial promotion of the shrine which the state will have to address in the larger interest of the people and ecology.

Mathur was indeed a great scholar. The vast literature he has left behind would not only be an inspiration for budding scholars but also a source of theoretical understanding.

References

Bose, NK. 1952. Current research projects in Indian Anthropology, *Man in India*, 32,3.

Bose, NK.1961. Introduction, In N.K.Bose (Ed): *Peasant Life in India: A Study in Unity and Diversity*, Anthropological Survey of India, Calcutta.

Bose, NK. 1963. *Fifty Years of Science in India: Progress of Anthropology and Archaeology*. Indian Science Congress Association, Calcutta.

Klaussen, AM.1965. *Kerala Fishermen and Indo-Norwegian Pilot Project*. Allen and Unwin, London.

Mathur, PRG. 1977. *Ecology, Technology, and Economy*. Indira Gandhi Rashtriya Manav Sangrahalaya. Bhopal, and Rawat Publications, Jaipur.

Mathur, PRG.1977. *The Mappila Fisherfolk of Kerala*. Kerala Historical Society, Trivandrum.

Mathur, PRG.1977. *Tribal Situation in Kerala*. Kerala Historical Society, Trivandrum.

Mishra, PK. 2018. *Tribal Heritage; An Overlooked Chapter of Indian History*, Aayu Publications, New Delhi.

Singh, KS. 1977. 'Foreword'. In PRG Mathur, *Tribal Situation in Kerala*. Kerala Historical Society, Trivandrum.

Sinha, SC. 1984. *Nirmal Kumar Bose: Scholar Wanderer*, National Book Trust, New Delhi.

Sinha, SC.1973. *Anthropology of Nirmal Kumar Bose*. N.K. Bose Memorial Foundation, Varanashi.

Chapter - 10

Life and Works of Dr Papia Banerjee

Abhishikta Ghosh Roy

Dr Papia Banerjee was a versatile scholar who worked on innumerable themes during her academic span. She had many caps that she donned that have nurtured students across the country. A silent motivator and worker, who never had any zeal for fame, but rather made impactful imprints for the generations to think over new areas. She was an innovationist who trademarked many links for modern anthropological techniques.

Born to an educationist family in 1934, Papia Banerjee was the third of eight siblings in the family. She hails from a very ordinary middle-class family located in Brahmanbaria, Comilla district (presently Bangladesh). Father was the Headmaster of Annada High School, Brahmanbaria. She grew up along with eight other siblings and made herself confident enough to make it through graduation and post-graduate degrees. During those days making up to college for a girl belonging to a middle-class family itself was challenging. She was the third among the siblings to make a mark for the family, Papia Banerjee completed her intermediate degree from Bir Bikram College, which is currently Tripura University. Later she graduated from City College, Kolkata with a distinction degree in biological sciences. The year 1962 was a revolutionary year that experienced the first award of a female in anthropology and Dr Papia Banerjee was credited for the same, being a diligent and intelligent scholar, her outcomes brought flying colours. She completed her doctoral thesis under the able guidance of the renowned anthropologist Dr S.S. Sarkar of Calcutta University. Her Ph.D. work was a celebrated one and the collections still add value to post-graduate students, 'Cephalic cranial correlation' on Contai skull was the topic.

Dr Banerjee had long-term acquaintances with stalwarts that always motivated her to conduct fieldwork among the Kadars of Kerala. The research article was hugely cited and published in Man in India, 1959 volume. She opted to work on areas that were less common among people and her work among the Juangs of Orissa was accredited and accepted by the anthropologists. All through her research, she was guided by Andre Betteile, S.S. Sarkar, and Nirmal Kumar Bose. She was one of the lucky souls to receive blessings and guidance from such eminent scholars.

Dr Banerjee's initial research focused on her desperation to disseminate knowledge reached levels where she attempted research for the first time in many areas. Anthropometric measurements among the Oraons have been studied by many scholars, noteworthy of them are Risley (1891), Basu, and Majumder (1941). Dr Banerjee first to study the Oraon females in the year 1956. Her paper mentions the lacunae in somatic data on female aborigines and the sexual diversification that remains absent from the country.

The eruption of teeth has always found its significance in anthropological studies. Her notable works always targeted the well-being of society at large. The eruption time of the deciduous teeth of the Bengalee children was noted and compared with the published material from other countries. It has been seen that the onset of eruption in the Bengalee children is appreciably late compared with the others (Japanese, Korean, American, and White). She nailed dental anthropology, today many scholars from archaeology and anthropology take a keen interest in understanding the same from various subjects. Dr Banerjee was always interested in areas which made her take a maiden attempt.

Birth weight is such a parameter that encompasses many biological and social events of the mother and the child. An attempt to understand the low birth weight of the newborns among the Bengalee population was a notable attempt that was published in the *American Journal of Physical Anthropology* in the year 1969. She beautifully mentioned how genetic, nongenetic, and epigenetic factors influence the birth weight of newborns. Approximately 50 years in between we are technically advanced and methodologies gained spectrum. To date, we have yet to experience research that can answer the possible outcomes that were reflected.

A contribution to the genetics of hypertrichosis of the ear rims was a joint publication wherein Geneticist, Curt Stern was the co-author. The report was the outcome of two data sets from two different regions of India. She extended the genetic study of Holandric genes and the pathbreaking work has been a clue to many research innovations. The research analyzed pedigrees from different populations to understand the Y-linked genetic transmissions.

During her distinguished tenure, she received many awards and honours. She extended her innovative research paradigm in Genetic Anthropology in various collaborative research programmes. The iconic anthropologist was always a silent scholar and kept the zeal for anthropological research alive.

She was highly influenced and was closely associated with luminaries like N.K. Bose and P.K. Bhowmick. Dr Banerjee remains one of the women anthropologists worth mentioning.

December 9, 2011, Kolkata witnessed the most horrific incident. AMRI Hospital, Kolkata was under fire. A few days before the incident she was admitted with cerebral attack and was placed in NICU, fourth floor of the hospital. At the age of 79 years, when she was severely ill, fire gasped her to almighty. It's often said that a fighter always fights to the death, the pathetic demise shook the entire fraternity.

Her contemporaries, colleagues, and students share her noteworthy heroics that assumed a source of enlightenment to the minds of many. It feels aghast that no lecture series, seminars, or webinars keep the ideas alive by sharing the repository of knowledge she left behind. The whole fraternity of anthropology and biological sciences remains indebted to her family and all the students and colleagues for the remembrance through which she is learned and her ideas are disseminated.

Chapter - 11

V. N. Misra: A Doyen of Indian Archaeology

A.R. Sankhyan

It is hard to recapitulate Dr Virendra Nath Misra (hereafter referred to as VNM) and his extremely hectic life, extensive and intensive varied types of activities, and research works in a very concise form. He was a running institution in himself, and many of his Ph.D. students and other scholars have showered praises on him. My interactions with VNM at different places impressed me with his simplicity, loving and caring nature, and great scholarship.

VNM came from a rural background, born in the small village of Khandauli in Farrukhabad district of Uttar Pradesh on 17th August 1935. His farming family had little resources to support his education. But because of his hard-working and pleasing nature, his teachers supported and encouraged him to pursue his studies. He was the first student from his village to pass the high school. His Hindi teacher Pt. B.N. Shastri encouraged and supported him to study Visharad in Hindi Sahitya Sammelan from Sanskrit Vidyalaya Allahabad. VNM secured first division in it, and later also passed the Prathama Certificate examination in Sanskrit from Government Sanskrit College, Benaras, winning a four-year Govt. scholarship to pursue further studies in Sanskrit. However, K.N. Sharma, Head of the Sociology Department at DAV College, influenced him to study Sociology along with History and English literature for his B.A. degree. He did so in 1955 with distinction. Then, he studied Anthropology as an M.A. student at

Lucknow University under Professor D.N. Majumdar getting a two-year' Bursary scholarship. VNM got the degree in 1957 in the first division with a Gold Medal. Being a compulsory part of the M.A. degree syllabus, VNM carried out two-week fieldwork in the tribal village in Mirzapur district. After his M.A. degree Majumdar asked him to conduct two months of fieldwork among the Austro-Asiatic-speaking Gond, Kharwar, Chero, and Korwa tribes. Then Majumdar appointed him as a Lecturer in the Anthropology Department to teach both Social Anthropology including Prehistoric Archaeology. Majumdar desired VNM to get training in prehistory from Deccan College, Pune, and come back to teach this branch. For this Deccan College offered VNM a monthly scholarship of Rs 80. He returned to Lucknow. And got a U.G.C. scholarship and continued teaching learning archaeology of the Mesolithic sites and rock paintings in Mirzapur, Uttar Pradesh on which he was also interested in doing a Ph.D. under H.D. Sankalia. But, since Professor G.R. Sharma was already working in the same area, Sankalia advised VNM to work in Rajasthan for a Ph.D. As that was almost a virgin for prehistory. VNM accepted and extended his research to Chittaurgarh in the Gambhiri and Berach rivers, including Pali in the Luni river basin. There he got stone tools with animal bones in stratified contexts, useful and helpful for reconstructing past climates and landforms. He conducted intensive fieldwork in the Banas river basin for three successive seasons and discovered Lower to Middle Palaeolithic tools; also explored four Mesolithic sites including a re-examination of the material of previous discoveries. All this formed a part of VNM's Ph.D. dissertation, entitled *Stone Age Cultures of Rajputana* submitted to Poona University under the guidance of H.D. Sankalia in July 1961, and he was awarded PhD degree in 1962. He also published an article on his thesis in the *Bulletin of the Deccan College*, Vol. 21 (1962).

During his fieldwork, while talking to the rural people, they didn't believe that such a highly qualified person was wasting his time and money picking up stones and animal bones! Of course, it is quite a general experience for all of us working in archaeology and paleontology. VNM faced many hardships, like disease-prone poor quality of drinking water in the desert of Rajasthan, including unavailability of proper food during the fieldwork.

During postgraduate and PhD studies, VNM continued to travel from Lucknow to Pune and back many times. VNM was committed to Majumdar to teach at Lucknow, and so had to decline Sankalia's offer of a Lecturer's job at the Deccan College. But, for the bad luck of VNM, Majumdar suddenly expired, and the department came under his colleague, K.S. Mathur. But Mathur like a gentleman kept Majumdar's promise to give the job to VNM at Lucknow University, and VNM joined as there as Lecturer (Assistant Professor) on 15th July 1961. After completing one academic year at Lucknow, VNM accepted Sankalia's new UGC lectureship at Deccan College owing to better research facilities and academic atmosphere. He joined Pune there on 26 July 1962. But, in between went to Calcutta for two months to study the Stone Age collections at the Indian Museum, especially the ground stone tools from North-east India, looking different from those of peninsular India.

From 1962 to 1981 VNM was on the staff of the Poona University Department of Archaeology, first as Lecturer (1962-68) and then as Reader and Head of the Department (1968-81). During this period, VNM also passed the certificate courses in French and German from Poona University, including a course in Russian. In 1981, he joined the Deccan College as a Professor of Prehistoric Archaeology. He became Joint Director in 1986 and Director in 1990, and retired on 31 August 2000.

Dr Mishra guided around 25 students for their PhDs. All of them occupied very high status in academics or administration Some of them are V Rami Reddy, Ms. Katy N. Frenchman, P.K. Thomas, Yasodhar Mathpal, D.R. Raju, Makhhan Lal, Jacob S. Jayaraj, S.C. Nanda, Ms. Zarine Cooper, Vijay Singh, Md. Shafiqul Alam, M.M. Hoque, J.S. Kharakwal, Ms. Bishnupriya Basak, Sunil Gupta, Shah Sufu Mustafizur Rahman, Ms. Mala Maiya Malla, B.S. Harishankar, Anup .R. Mishra, Balaram Tripathy, Ms. Shahida Ansari, Kurush Feroze Dalal, Abhijit Dandekar, Tama Panda, and Kumar Akhilesh

Research activities: Explorations in Gujarat and Rajasthan

First, he resumed his earlier fieldwork in Rajasthan, concentrating on the Berach basin in Mewar, the districts Udaipur, Chittaurgarh, and Bhilwara. He discovered several Lower and Middle Palaeolithic,

Microlithic, and Chalcolithic sites in the valleys of the Berach, Gambhiri, and Wagan rivers. Chalcolithic sites there belonged to the Ahar Culture, which included painted Black-and-Red Ware (BRW), and Tan Ware, with distinct Harappan affinity.

In 1966, VNM and L.S. Leshnik of the Heidelberg University, West Germany carried out extensive explorations in Rajasthan and Gujarat, mainly to test Leshnik's hypothesis that early agriculture may have begun in the foothill region of the Aravalli Mountains. During the explorations, apart from many small microlithic and later sites, they discovered two important Mesolithic sites at Tilwara in Barmer district in western Rajasthan and Bagor in Bhilwara district in eastern Rajasthan. As trial digs at these sites proved promising, in the following four years VNM excavated them on a larger scale jointly with the Department of Archaeology and Museums of the Rajasthan Government, Jaipur.

Tilwara excavation

Located on a low dune about two km away from the southern bank of the Luni River at the eastern edge of the Thar desert, showing just a two feet deposit that yielded geometric microlithic industry made on chert and quartz in the lower levels and microliths associated with wheel-made pottery and iron tools in the upper levels.

Bagor excavation

Located on a low dune on the left bank of the Kothari River, associated with Mahasati, where Rajput women committed sati (self-immolation). At Tilwara, the workers in the excavation hosted a feast of traditional Mewari dishes, accompanied by music and throwing of colour. During the Balathal excavation, he visited Bagor again, where the workers lifted him and danced with joy. The site Bagor remains the largest Mesolithic site excavated so far in India, showing the cultural sequence in three phases: the microlithic, followed by handmade poorly baked pottery decorated with incised designs, and three human burials with the body buried in a flexed position. This is followed by copper objects, clay pots, beads of semi-precious stones and bone, and animal bones. Phase III microlithic industry wheel-made pottery of the early historic period and iron tools appeared. Bagor was the first archaeological site in India from which entire animal bone material was collected by P.K. Thomas for his Ph.D. degree.

VNM presented his work of Bagor in 1969 at the 2nd International Conference of Asian Archaeology at Colombo, and also visited the famous Beli Lena Athula, Beli Lena Kitugala, and Batadomba Lena, and made friends with Siran Deraniagala.

Balathal excavation

Balathal was one of the nine sites of the Ahar Chalcolithic culture which VNM had discovered in Mewar during his 1962-64 explorations. In 1989, Vice-Chancellor of the Vidyapeeth, K.K. Vashisth invited VNM to deliver the Gourichand Hirachand Ojha Memorial lecture and desired to establish an Archaeology Department in his University. VNM proposed to train their staff by carrying out a joint excavation with the Deccan College and the Balathal was selected owing to its Ahar culture. It was horizontally excavated for seven seasons (1994-2000). The finds from the excavations produced evidence of two cultural periods, viz. Chalcolithic and Early Historic. The Balathal people had contact with the Harappan people of Gujarat, contemporary with Early and Mature Harappan cultures, c.3700-3620 BC to 2200-1800 BC. Balathal people cultivated wheat, barley, green gram, black gram, common pea, jujube, and millets and domestication of cattle, buffalo, sheep, goat, and pig. Evidence of ironworking and a rich and varied assemblage of iron tools and weapons, including several terracotta seals with Brahmi script have been found in this period.

Bhimbetka excavations

In 1970, Homi Bhabha Fellowship was awarded to VNM to study European prehistory, and he visited Israel, Italy, France, Germany, the U.K., the Netherlands, Denmark, and Czechoslovakia for a large number of Archaeology Departments, Museums, and excavations, participated in Francois Bordes' excavation at Pech de l'Aze and Henry de Lumley's excavation at Grotte de Lazaret in France.

He returned to India with a determination to look for and excavate a cave site, Bhimbetka, discovered in 1972 by V.S. Wakankar. H.D. Sankalia asked VNM to undertake the excavation on behalf of the

Deccan College at Bhimbetka hill shelters are archaeological site complex in the Raisen district of Madhya Pradesh.

The Bhimbetka (70°37'E: 22°50'N) hill is situated about 45 km south of Bhopal 35 km north of Hoshangabad, and about two km south of the tribal village of Bhiyanpur, mainly the Gond, who extensively exploit the wild plant food resources of this hill. This village is located on the southern side of the Mumbai-Delhi rail line and highway running parallel to it. The Bhimbetka Hill possesses over 200 caves and rock shelters, some contain evidence of occupation by Stone Age man, and almost all of them contain paintings dating from the Stone Age to the historical period. Several other hills in the vicinity of Bhimbetka also contain caves and rock shelters totaling 1000. The caves and rock shelters have been formed by natural weathering in the soft Vindhyan sandstone. I and my associates visited Bhimbetka several times during our Narmada Valley Explorations conducted during the mid-1980s, 1990s, and 2005-2010. We collected Palaeolithic to Microlithic tools, which could date to over one lakh years.

One of the shelters at Bhimbetka overlooking the green valley is situated about two km from the road, and the excavation team had to walk a two km distance to the site. At that time there was no well-defined path to the hill and the camp team hired bullock carts to carry the equipment.

V.S.Wakankar and Yashodhar Mathpal classified the shelters into a three-tiered scheme. The first tier consists of eight main groups or areas which have been numbered I-VIII. Each area has been divided into subareas or clusters which have been numbered A, B, C, etc. And in each cluster, the shelters have been numbered 1, 2, 3, etc. Thus, each shelter bears a three-tier number, for example, IIIF-23. In 1972 V.S. Wakankar began excavation at the site and dug in several shelters for five seasons. In 1973, VN Misra, assisted by research scholars like Yashodhar Mathpal, etc. and the technical staff, dug three shelters, namely IIIF-23, IIIF-13, and IIB-33 for five seasons. VNM regards Bhimbetka as the most memorable of his excavation camps.

Notable foreign archaeologists, like Henry de Lumley and M.A. de Lumley and J.R. Lukacs have visited the excavations. In December 1978, VNM, under all odds, organised a visit of about 50 international archaeologists to the site. The major findings of the excavations in three shelters at XIIa. III F-23 yielded an unbroken cultural sequence from Late Acheulian through Mesolithic to Chalcolithic, and finally to Iron Age.

In 1979, he went to Greece under the Indo-Greek cultural exchange programme, and saw Studies in Prehistory and Ethnoarchaeology of South Asia.

Narmada valley excavations

Given thick alluvial deposits of Middle Pleistocene to Holocene with rich mammalian fossils, and Palaeolithic and Mesolithic artifacts found particularly in its central part between Narsinghpur and Hoshangabad, since the 1830s, VNM was also attracted in the mid-1960s to lay hands on human remains, for which until 1980s only Arun Sonakia, succeeded accidentally in getting one partial skullcap in December 1982, reported in 1985 by Lumley and Sonakia (1985). In 1986, H.D. Sankalia proposed a 5-year project in Narmada Valley involving VNM, S.N. Rajaguru, and G.L. Badam, including other participants. The aim was to look for human fossils, reconstruct the palaeoclimatic and palaeoenvironmental history of the region, and relate stone tool industries with palaeoclimatic phases. They focused on Narsinghpur, Devakachar- Samnapur - Kerpani sites located on the Narmada River. They excavated and discovered several Palaeolithic and Mesolithic tools, notably from the Samnapur exposed section, yielding an assemblage of flakes, a variety of scrapers, knives, and denticulates (without bifaces) in primary context as indicated by the cores and flaking debris along with animal fossils, belonging to the Middle Palaeolithic to Upper Palaeolithic period.

Unfortunately, the Deccan College scholars and the Geological Survey of India palaeontologists couldn't succeed in getting any human fossils before and after Sonakia. Perhaps luck would favour the Anthropological Survey of India (AnSI) under the Narmada Project during the 1980s, and early1990s, and from 2005-2010, the early phase explorations yielded one complete human right and partial left clavicle and a partial 9th rib reported in the *Journal of Human Evolution* and *Current Science* in 1997 and 2005. From the last phase (2005-2010) collections, the author of this chapter scrutinised the Namada fossil collection and discovered 11 more human fossil bones, which include, femora, humeri, and sacra, first reported in 2017.

In addition, VNM participated in the prehistoric explorations in the excavations at Neolithic Tekkalakota (Karnataka), Tripuri (M.P.) under Sankalia, including the enigmatic copper hoards as well Painted Grey Ware (PGW) In U.P. He also explored PGW and related sites at Kampil, Farrukhabad, and Sankisa in Farrukhabad district, Jajmau in Kanpur district, and Shampur in Hordoi district.

Prof. Misra - A great organizer

Some more important of these may be mentioned here. In 1964, H.D. Sankalia organised the first national seminar on *'Prehistory and Proto-history of India'*, at Deccan College with VNM as Secretary. Forty archaeologists were invited to participate. The proceedings were edited by VNM and M.S. Mate and were published by the Deccan College in 1965 under the title, *Indian Prehistory: 1964*. The second was the *Symposium on Indo-Pacific Prehistory* 1978. The proceedings of the symposium, edited by VNM and Peter Bellwood, were published under the title of *Recent Advances in Indo-Pacific Prehistory* by Oxford-IBH, New Delhi in 1985. VNM was a member of the National Organizing Committee of the *10th International Congress of Anthropological and Ethnological Sciences* (ICAES), held in New Delhi in December 1978. 122 scholars from 13 countries participated in it. *World Archaeological Congress – 3 (WAC- 3)* 1994 was hurriedly founded in 1986 out of a stormy split in the International Union of Prehistoric and Protohistoric Sciences (IUPPS). There was lots of chaos and a group of scholars were divided after the Babri Masjid demolition. I witnessed the chaotic situation in Delhi. Somehow, VNM managed the situation as he was given the responsibility of Secretary General for organising it in Ashoka Hotel, New Delhi. He was also the ex-officio convener of all the committees, and it was a stupendous task for him to prepare the agenda and minutes of the meetings of all the committees and send them to the members, spent almost a year traveling frequently to Delhi. Because of the adverse propaganda in the Indian Press, the President of India who had earlier agreed to inaugurate the Congress declined to do so at the last moment. Altogether, the conference turned Virendra Nath Misra to test in such a chaotic situation.

The Indian Archaeological Society (IAS), The Indian Society for Prehistoric and Quaternary Studies (ISPQS), Pune, and the Indian History and Culture Society (IHCS), New Delhi organised the joint conference of the societies under the leadership of VNM at the Deccan College to observe the Diamond Jubilee of the College as a Research Institute. It was one of the most widely attended conferences.

The Indian Archaeological Society (IAS) was founded in Varanasi in 1966 at the initiative of Prof. A.K. Narain, and it started studies in the prehistory of South Asia, organizing conferences and publishing its yearly journal, *Puratattva*. Later, in 1975, the *Indian Society for Prehistoric and Quaternary Studies* (ISPQS) was established to promote research in totality. It started its journal, *Man and Environment* in 1977 with VNM as Editor and also General Secretary during 1981-2000. It became the main archaeology journal in South Asia. VNM established the *H.D. Sankalia Young Archaeologist Award* through the Society, including others, the *Malti Nagar Award for Ethnoarchaeology*, and the *R.K. Sharma Award for Excellence in Archaeology*.

At his felicitation at the Societies conference at Tirupati in 2003, VN Misra's contributions as anthropologist – archaeologist received great recognition and highlight. VNM had firm contention in the *'Prehistoric roots of Indian society'* visible in the lifeways of the rural and tribal people. He stressed that the present society can better be understood through archaeology. VNM acknowledged the great contributions of his teachers not only to archaeology but for encouraging, guiding, and promoting his education and research career. He particularly mentioned Pandit Brahmanand Shastri, Prof. K.N. Sharma, D.N. Majumdar, and H.D. Sankalia playing significant roles in his life and academic journey and inspiring him to face great challenges. He particularly appreciated his colleague S.N. Rajaguru for his work on the Rajasthan and Narmada Valley projects and for being honest unassuming and extremely devoted to his work. He also acknowledged many of his competent and dedicated colleagues and students and many leading archaeologists from India and outside. He is also happy that his bright, honest, and hardworking students doing doctoral research under his supervision assumed archaeology as a professional career, and got good jobs.

VNM happily acknowledged many caring friends, viz., Vishwa Mohan, P.K. Tewari, S.P. Gupta, D.P. Agrawal, late K.T.M. Hegde, S.C. Gupte. He also felt extremely grateful to his wife who has taken care of the home, leaving him free to pursue his research, and cheerfully endured long periods.

VNM as a human being

By temperament, VNM was simple, unassuming, and informal, and least conscious of his academic or administrative status. On his letterhead or visiting card he has never used Dr or Prof. before his name or academic degrees after it. As head of the Department of Archaeology and director of the Institute, he was easily accessible to everybody who wanted to see him – be it a student, lower class employee, or any visitor. He would offer a chair to every person who went to see him and hated to keep people standing, as is common with administrators in India. He would also offer tea/coffee to every visitor and by giving company to them ended up drinking several cups every day. His home has been as welcome a place as his office, and students and staff members were free to visit him at any hour even on holidays. Even after his retirement quite a few students and colleagues continue to visit him. As Deccan College did not have a guest house, his home served as a guest house for many visitors to the College. He would freely mix with students and employees irrespective of their status, particularly during festivals like *Holi* and the immersion of Ganesh idols. VNM is always polite and respectful to others, in particular to those less privileged than him, and is very conscious of not hurting the feelings of anybody. He is particularly respectful to women, irrespective of their age or status. He has deep respect for his teachers, elders, and people who have helped him in some way or the other. He feels most happy in the company of simple and innocent people like the workers in his excavations and informants in ethnographic inquiries. VNM also derives happiness by being able to help others and has helped many needy people by lending them money, students in getting fellowships and grants, and colleagues in getting funding for conferences, etc. In return, he has received plenty of kindness, help, and hospitality from numerous students and professional colleagues all over the country and outside, and he greatly cherishes the consideration shown to him by so many people. Being born in a village on the bank of a large river,

Ramganga, VNM learned swimming at a very early age and is very fond of it. If he sees a river or lake, he can't resist jumping into it. When he was digging at Samnapur in the late 1980s, he had to cross the Narmada twice every day by boat. In the evening while returning to his camp he will invariably swim in the river. He has also been fond of walking.

Up to almost the age of sixty years, he used to play badminton every day. In his youth, he was also fond of playing chess. Unfortunately, from 2004 he was not keeping good health, which restricted his movements, but continued reading writing, and answering e-mails and letters. Unfortunately, we lost VN Misra, on 31st October 2015, at the age of 80 years. Numerous newspapers and scholars, both in India and abroad gave their tributes to him.

Important publications

Books

1965. *Indian Prehistory*: Poona: Deccan College (with MS Mate).

1965. *Pre and Proto-history of the Berach Basin, South Rajasthan*. Poona: Deccan College.

1967. *Bagor and Tilwara: Late Mesolithic Cultures of Northwest India*. Vol. I: *The Human Skeletal Remains*. Poona: Deccan College (with JR Lukacs, KAR Kennedy).

1978. *Prehistoric Man and his Art at Bhimbetka, Central India*. Poona (with Y Mathpal, M Nagar).

1985. *Recent Advances in Indo-Pacific Prehistory*. Delhi: Oxford-IBH (with P Bellwood).

1992 *Indus Civilisation,* a special number of the Eastern Anthropologist. Lucknow: Ethnographic and Folk Culture Society.

Research papers

1962 Palaeolithic industry of the Banas, Eastern Rajputana, *Journal of the Asiatic Society of Bombay*, 34-35: 138-160.

1962 Problems of terminology in Indian prehistory, *Eastern Anthropologist*, 15,2: 112-124.

1962 Palaeolithic culture of Western Rajputana, *Bulletin of the Deccan College Research Institute*, 21: 86-156.

1963 Two stone age sites on the River Chambal, Rajasthan (joint), *Bulletin of the Deccan College Research Institute*, 22:156-169.

1964 Palaeoliths from district Udaipur Rajasthan, *Journal of the Asiatic Society of Bombay*, 36-37: 55-59.

1965 Govindgarh, A palaeolithic site in Western Rajasthan, *Journal of the Asiatic Society of Bombay*, 38: 205-208.

1965 Mesolithic phase in the prehistory of India. In V.N. Misra and M.S. Mate (Ed.), *Indian Prehistory*: 1964, pp. 57-85. Poona: Deccan College.

1966 Stoneage research in Rajasthan – A review. In D. Sen and A.K. Ghosh (Eds.), *Studies in Prehistory: Robert Bruce Foote Memorial Volume*, pp. 122-130. Calcutta: Firma K.L. Mukhopadhyaya.

1967 Prehistory and protohistory. In P.J. Chinmulgund and V.V. Mirashi (Eds.), *Review of Indological Research in Last Seventy-five Years*, pp. 351-425. Poona: Charitrakosh Mandal.

1968. Middle stoneage in Rajasthan. In Francois Bordes and D. de. Sonneville-Bordes (Eds.), *La Prehistoire: Problems et Tendances*, pp. 295-302. Paris: Centre National de la Recherche Scientifique.

1968 Late stoneage in Rajasthan. In *Proceedings of the Rajasthan History Congress*, First Session, pp. 16-22. Jaipur.

1969 Early village communities of the Banas basin, Rajasthan. In, M.C. Pradhan et al (Eds.), *Anthropology and Archaeology: Essays in Memory of Verrier Elwin*, pp. 295-310. Bombay: Oxford University Press.

1970 Cultural significance of three copper arrow-heads from Rajasthan, India, *Journal of Near Eastern Studies*, 29, 4: 221-232.

1970. Evidence for a new chalcolithic culture in South Rajasthan, *Indian Antiquary* (Third Series),4,1-4: 85-95.

1970 Excavation in Rajasthan, *Quarterly Journal of the Mythic Society*, 18,1-4: 9-16.

1971 Two microlithic sites in Rajasthan – A preliminary investigation, *Eastern Anthropologist*, 24,3: 237-288.

1971 Two late mesolithic settlements in Rajasthan – A brief review of investigations, *Poona University Journal* (Humanities), 35: 59-79.

1971 Stone objects from Navdatoli. In, H.D. Sankalia, S.B. Deo and Z.D. Ansari (Eds): *Chalcolithic Navdatoli*, pp. 323-350 Poona: Deccan College.

1972 Prehistoric burials from Bagor, Rajasthan. In, S.B. Deo (Ed.), *Archaeological Congress and Seminar Papers*, pp. 58-65. Nagpur: Nagpur University.

1972 Evolution of palaeolithic cultures in India In, Francois Bordes (Ed.), *The Origin of Homo Sapiens*, pp. 116-120. Paris: UNESCO.

1973 Problems of palaeo-ecology, palaeo-climate, and chronology of the microlithic cultures of Western India. In, D.P. Agrawal and A. Ghosh (Eds.), *Radiocarbon and Indian Archaeology*, pp. 58-72. Bombay: Tata Institute of Fundamental Research.

1973 Twenty-five years of Indian prehistory (1947-1972) – A review of research (Joint) In, K.S. Mathur and S.C. Varma (Eds.), *Man and Society*, pp. 1-54. Lucknow: Ethnographic and Folk Culture Society.

1973 Bagor – A late mesolithic settlement in north-west India, *World Archaeology*, 5,1: 92-110.

1973 A new prehistoric ceramic from Rajasthan, *East and West*, 23,3-4: 295-305.

1973 New light on the mesolithic period in India from excavations at Bagor in Rajasthan, *The Researcher*, 12-13:1-14.

1974 Archaeological and ethnographic evidence for the hafting and use of microliths and related tools, *Puratattva*, 7: 3-12.

1974 History and archaeology – Need for a new understanding, *Prachya Pratibha*, 2,1: 8-14.

1976 The acheulian Industry of rock-shelter III F-23 at Bhimbetka, Central India, *Puratattva*, 8: 13-36.

1976 Ecological adaptations during the terminal stone age in western and central India. In, K.A.R. Kennedy and G. Possehl

(Eds.), *Ecological Backgrounds of South Asian Prehistory*, pp. 28-51. Ithaca: Cornell University.

1976 Prehistory and palaeoenvironment in Rajasthan. In, D.P. Agrawal and B.M. Pande (Eds.), *Archaeology and Palaeoenvironment in Western India*, pp. 31-54. New Delhi: Concept.

1976 Prehistoric background of Rajasthan (Joint). In, R. Subrahmanyam and N. Ramesan (Eds.), *Somasekhara Sarma Commemoration Volume*, pp. 345-59. Hyderabad: Government of Andhra Pradesh.

1976 Evidence of cultural contact between terminal stone-age hunter-gatherers and contemporary farmers. In U.V. Singh (Ed.), *Archaeological Congress and Seminar*: 1972, pp. 151-161. Kurukshetra: Kurukshetra University.

1977 Evolution of the pattern of human settlement in the arid and semi-arid region. In, P.L. Jaiswal, R. Singh, N.N. Chhabra and K. Sundararaman (Eds.), *Desertification and its Control*, pp. 10-24. New Delhi: Indian Council of Agricultural Research.

1978 Prehistoric cave art of Bhimbetka, Central India. In, C. Pearson (Ed.), *Conservation of Rock Art*, pp. 69-70. Canberra.

1978 Acheulian industry of Bhimbetka, Central India. *Bulletin of the Indo-Pacific Prehistory Association*, 1: 130-173.

1978 Explorations in Ajmer and Jaipur Districts, Rajasthan, *Man and Environment*, II: 74.

1979 Rock art of Bhimbetka region, Central India (Joint). *Man and Environment,* III: 27-33.

1980 Prehistory and palaeoenvironment of Jayal, Western Rajasthan (Joint). *Man and Environment*, 4: 19-31.

1980 Palaeoclimate, stratigraphy, and prehistory in North and West Rajasthan (Joint) *Proceedings of the Indian Academy of Sciences*, 89, 1: 51-66.

1980 Quaternary studies in Rajasthan – Preliminary results (Joint) *Recent Researches in Geology*, 9: 186-189.

1980 The acheulian industry of rock-shelter IIIF-23 at Bhimbetka, Central India – A preliminary study, *Australian Archaeology*, 8: 63-106.

1980 Multiple evidence for climatic change in Rajasthan (Joint) In, H.S. Mann (Ed.), *Arid Zone Research and Development*, pp. 1-18. Jodhpur: Scientific Publishers.

1981 The prehistoric rock art of Bhimbetka, Central India, *Journal of the National Centre for the Performing Arts*,10,1: 1-16.

1981 Dental mutilations from prehistoric India (Joint) *Current Anthropology*, 22,3: 256-86.

1981 Palaeoclimatic inferences from the behaviour of radiocarbon dates of carbonates from sand-dunes of Rajasthan (Joint). *Proceedings of the Indian Academy of Sciences*, 90,2: 155-160

1981 The microlithic industry of Bagor, Rajasthan (Joint), In, V.S. Srivastava (Ed.), *Cultural Contours of India*, pp. 6-11. Delhi: Abhinav.

1982 The evolution of blade elements in the stone industries of Bhimbetka, Central India. In, R.K. Sharma (Ed.), *Indian Archaeology: New Perspectives,* pp. 7-13. Delhi: Agam Prakashan.

1982 Acheulian occupation and evolving landscape around Didwana in the Thar desert, India (Joint). *Man and Environment*, 6: 72-86.

1983 Acheulian occupation at Singi Talav in the Thar desert: A preliminary report on 1982 excavation (Joint). *Man and Environment*, 7: 112-130.

1983 Geomorphology, Late quaternary stratigraphy and palaeoclimatology of the Thar dune field (Joint). *Zeitschrift fur Geomorphologie* (N.F.), 45: 117-151.

1983 Further light on lower palaeolithic occupation and palaeoenvironment in semi-arid Zone of Rajasthan (Joint) *Puratattva*, 11: 11-18.

1983 Environment during the quaternary period in Western India (Joint). *Proceedings of the Workshop on Problems of Deserts in India*. Jaipur: Geological Survey of India.

1984 Climate as a factor in the rise and fall of Harappan civilisation: Evidence from Rajasthan and beyond. In, B.B. Lal and S.P. Gupta (Eds.), *Frontiers of the Indus Civilisation*, pp. 461-489. New Delhi: Books and Books.

1984 Evolution of environment and human settlement in the Thar desert, India: A review of the evidence (Joint). *Proceedings of the Indo-US Workshop on the Arid Zone Research*, pp. 1-17. Jodhpur: Central Arid Zone Research Institute.

1985. The acheulian succession at Bhimbetka, Central India. In, V.N. Misra and P. Bellwood (Eds.), *Recent Advances in Indo-Pacific Prehistory*, pp. 35-47. New Delhi: Oxford - IBH.

1985 Microlithic industries of India. In, V.N. Misra and P. Bellwood (Eds.), *Recent Advances in Indo-Pacific Prehistory*, pp. 111-122. New Delhi: Oxford-IBH.

1986 Bhimbetka: Reflections of life in cave art. *Science Age*, 4,6: 17-26.

1986 A note on the mineralogical study of some sand-dunes from the Thar desert. (Joint). *Bulletin of the Deccan College Research Institute*, 45: 35-46.

1986 Environnement et culture de l'homme prehistorique dans le desert du Thar, Rajasthan, Inde (Joint). *L'Anthropologie,* 90, 3: 407-437.

1986 Handaxe assemblages from the Didwana region, Thar desert, India: A metrical analysis (Joint). *Proceedings of the Prehistoric Society*, 52: 189-214.

1987 Evolution of the landscape and human adaptation in the Thar desert. Presidential Address, Anthropology and Archaeology Section of Indian Science Congress, Bangalore, *Proceedings of the 74th Indian Science Congress*, Part II: 1-24.

1987 History of environment and man in the Thar desert (Joint). *Indologica Jaipurensia*, I: 17-31.

1987 Middle pleistocene adaptations in India. In, Olga Soffer (Ed.), *Pleistocene Old World: Regional Perspectives*, pp. 99-114. New York: Plenum Press.

1988 History of environment and man in the Thar desert (Joint). *Journal of Ecological Society*, I: 7-16.

1988 Late middle pleistocene environment and acheulian culture around Didwana, Rajasthan (Joint). *Proceedings of the Indian National Science Academy*, 54, A,3: 425-438.

1988 Significance of vertebrate remains from archaeological sites in the arid and semi-arid zones of Northwest India.

In, P.K. Ghosh and Ishwar Prakash (Eds.), *Ecophysiology of Desert Vertebrates*, pp. 35-57. Jodhpur: Scientific Publishers.

1989 Radiometric dating of a quaternary dune section, Didwana, Rajasthan (Joint). *Man and Environment*, 13: 19-22.

1989 Hunter-gatherers in an agrarian setting: The nineteenth-century situation in the Ganga plains (Joint). *Man and Environment*, 13: 65-78.

1989 Stoneage India: An ecological perspective, *Man and Environment* 14,1: 17-64.

1989 Mesolithic occupation around Dhansura, district Sabarkantha, Gujarat (Joint) *Man and Environment*, 14,1: 123-128.

1989 Comparative study of three series of handaxes – One from Rajasthan and two from Andhra Pradesh (Joint). *Bulletin of the Deccan College Research Institute* 49: 137-144.

1989 Van Vagris: Nomadic hunters of Western Rajasthan. In, S.C. Tiwari (Ed.) *Changing Perspectives of Anthropology in India*, pp. 285-311. New Delhi: Today and Tomorrows Printers and Publishers.

1989 Mesolithic cultures. In, A. Ghosh (Ed.), *Encyclopaedia of Indian Archaeology*, Vol. I: Subjects, pp. 37-43. New Delhi: Munshiram Manoharlal.

1989 Banas culture. In, A. Ghosh (Ed.), *Encyclopaedia of Indian Archaeology*, Vol. I: Subjects, pp. 96-98. New Delhi: Munshiram Manoharlal.

1989 Deserts. In, A. Ghosh (Ed.), *Encyclopaedia of Indian Archaeology*, Vol. I: Subjects, pp. 197-201. New Delhi: Munshiram Manoharlal.

1989 Rock art (Joint). In, A. Ghosh (Ed.), *Encyclopaedia of Indian Archaeology*, Vol. I: Subjects, pp. 279-284. New Delhi: Munshiram Manoharlal.

1989 Ecology and settlement pattern. In, A. Ghosh (Ed.), *Encyclopaedia of Indian Archaeology*, Vol. I: Subjects, pp. 285-287. New Delhi: Munshiram Manoharlal.

1989. Bagor. In, A. Ghosh (Ed.), *Encyclopaedia of Indian Archaeology*, Vol. II: A Gazetteer of Explored and Excavated Sites, pp. 35-37. New Delhi: Munshiram Manoharlal.

1989 Palaeoenvironment and prehistory of the Thar desert, Rajasthan, India (Joint). In, Karen Frifelt and Per Sorensen (Eds.), *South Asian Archaeology* 1985, pp. 296-320. Copenhagen: Scandinavian Institute of Asian Studies.

1989 Human adaptations to the changing landscape of the Indian arid zone during the quaternary period. In, J.M. Kenoyer (Ed.), *Old Problems and New Perspectives in the Archaeology of South Asia*, Wisconsin Archaeological Reports, Volume 2, pp. 3-20. Madison: University of Wisconsin-Madison.

1989 Collection of non-utilitarian objects by Homo erectus in India (Joint). In, Giacomo Giacobini (Ed.) *Hominidae: Proceedings of the Second International Congress of Human Palaeontology*. Milan: Jaca Books.

1990 Geoarchaeology of the palaeolithic site at Samnapur in the Central Narmada Valley (Joint). *Man and Environment* 15,1: 107-116.

1990 Palaeolithic phase in India, *Ancient Ceylon* 7,2: 101-149.

1990 The Kanjars – A hunting-gathering community of the Ganga Valley, Uttar Pradesh (Joint). *Man and Environment* 15,2: 71-88.

1990 The Van Vagris – "Lost" hunters of the Thar desert, Rajasthan, *Man, and Environment* 15,2: 89-108.

1990 Prehistoric cultural stages in the middle Son Valley, *The Indian Historical Review* 14,1-2: 252-262.

1990 Further research in the prehistory and quaternary geology of the Narmada Valley (Joint). In, N.C. Ghosh and S. Chakrabarti (Eds.), *Adaptation and Other Essays*, pp. 53-59. Santiniketan: Visva-Bharati.

1992 Archaeology and tribes. In, A.K. Singhvi and Amal Kar (Eds.) *The Thar Desert in Rajasthan: Land, Man and Environment*, pp. 85-94. Bangalore: Geological Survey of India.

1992 Research on the Indus civilisation: A brief review. In, V.N. Misra (Ed.), *Indus Civilisation Special Number of the Eastern Anthropologist* 45,1-2: 1-19.

1992 Quantitative composition and functional aspect of the palaeolithic assemblages of rock shelter IIIF-23 at Bhimbetka (Joint). *Man and Environment* 17,2: 21-34.

1993 The Pardhis: A hunting-gathering community of Central and Western India (Joint). *Man and Environment* 18,1: 115-140.

1993 Professor S.M. Katre as I knew him in the Deccan College, *Bulletin of the Deccan College Research Institute* 51-52: 31-38.

1993 Terracotta bull figurines from Marmi: A chalcolithic settlement in Chittorgarh district, Rajasthan (Joint). *Man and Environment* 18,2: 149-152.

1994 Survival of the hunting-gathering tradition in the Ganga plains and Central India (Joint). In, Bridget Allchin (Ed.) *Living Traditions: Studies in the Ethnoarchaeology of South Asia*, pp. 169-192.

1994 Indus civilisation and the Rigvedic Sarasvati. In, Asko Parpola and Petteri Koskikallio (Eds.), South Asian Archaeology: 1993. *Proceedings of the Twelfth International Conference of the European Association of South Asian Archaeologists*, pp. 511-525. Helsinki: Suomalainen Tiedeakatemia.

1995 Evolution of environment and culture in the Rajasthan desert during the late quarternary. In, Eileen Johnson (Ed.) *Ancient Peoples and Landscapes*, pp. 77-103. Lubbock, Texas: Texas Tech University Press.

1995 Geoarchaeology of the Thar desert, Northwest India. In, S. Wadia, R. Korisettar and V.S. Kale (Eds.) *Quaternary Environments and Geoarchaeology of India: Essays in Honour of Professor S.N. Rajaguru*, pp. 210-230. Bangalore: Geological Society of India.

1995 Excavations at Balathal: Their contribution to the chalcolithic and iron age cultures of Mewar, Rajasthan (Joint). *Man and Environment* 20,1: 57-80.

1996 Indus civilisation and the Rigvedic Sarasvati. In, *Second International Congress Proceedings*, pp.125-142. Bombay: H.R. Cama Oriental Institute.

1996 Palaeoenvironment and prehistory of the Thar desert, Rajasthan, India (Joint). In, B.L. Bhadani and Dwijendra Tripathi (Eds.), *Facets of a Marwar Historian: Aspects of India's Social and Economic History* (A Volume in Honour of Shri Govind Agarwal), pp. 99-130. Jaipur: Publication Scheme.

1997 Balathal: A chalcolithic settlement in Mewar, Rajasthan, India: Results of first three seasons excavations. South Asian Archaeology, *South Asian Studies*, 13: 251-273.

1997 Early man and his environment in Central India. *Journal of the Palaeontological Society of India* 42: 1-18.

1997 Excavations at Balathal, district Udaipur, Rajasthan (1995-97), with special reference to chalcolithic architecture (Joint). *Man and Environment* 22,2: 35-59.

1997 Further light on lower palaeolithic occupation and palaeoenvironment in semi-arid zone of Rajasthan (Joint). In, V.D. Misra and J.N. Pal (Eds.), *Indian Prehistory 1980 (Proceedings of the Seminar on Indian Prehistory and Protohistory* held in the Department of Ancient History, Culture, and Archaeology, University of Allahabad, November 29 - December 03, 1980), pp. 51-60. Allahabad: Department of Ancient History, Culture and Archaeology, University of Allahabad.

1997 From tribe to caste: An ethnoarchaeological perspective (Joint). In, Dev Nathan (Ed.) *From Tribe to Caste*, pp. 136-166. Shimla: Indian Institute of Advanced Study.

1998 Hunter-gatherers in Ganga plains (Joint). In, H.S. Saksena, B.R.K. Shukla, P.K. Tewari and P.N. Sharma (Eds.) *Perspectives in Tribal Development: Focus on Uttar Pradesh*, pp. 141-47. Lucknow: Ethnographic and Folk Culture Society.

1999 Pottery. In, B.V. Subbarayappa (Ed.) *Chemistry and Chemical Techniques in India (History of Science, Philosophy, and Culture in Indian Civilisation*, Vol. IV, Part I, pp. 223-244. New Delhi: Centre for Studies in Civilisations.

2001 Archaeological evidence of early modern human occupation in South Asia, in P.V. Tobias, M.A. Raath, J. Moggi-Cecchi and G.A. Doyle (Eds.) *Humanity from African Naissance to coming Millenia,* pp 223-230. Firenze: Ferenze University Press.

Chapter - 12

Life and Anthropological Studies of Prof. Keshari N. Sahay

P. Dash Sharma

My first meeting with Dr Keshari Nandan Sahay at Ranchi happened in 1970 November when I visited Ranchi on deputation from the Anthropological Survey of India, Mysore Station, for teaching and a research assignment at Ranchi. I was introduced to Dr K. N. Sahay by Dr Asesh Kumar Haldar at that time with whom I had some acquaintance through a common friend. Hefty and tall Dr Sahay was a very soft-spoken, sober, and malleable person. In later years I found him more religiously inclined and introvert, and he was also a member of a few religious and yoga societies in Ranchi. Dr K. N. Sahay was a man with varied interests. He has written novels and poems in Hindi and Maghi language, and dwelled in spiritualism and yoga, apart from anthropological research, particularly on Christianity and culture change among tribals of Chotanagpur. I found in him a steadfast person in academics and spiritualism.

Dr Keshari N. Sahay was born in Muzaffarpur (Bihar) in 1935. He did his schooling at Patna from Miller School and did his graduation from Gaya College, Bihar. After his graduation study, he came over to Ranchi for higher studies at Ranchi College where postgraduate classes were held during the years in 50s.

Keshari Nandan Sahay (1935-2013) received his MA degree in Anthropology in 1956 from Bihar University, studying at the Postgraduate Department of Anthropology at Ranchi College. Ranchi

University was founded in July 1961 severing Bihar University. After his post-graduation studies in anthropology, Mr K. N. Sahay worked as a Research Assistant in two large-scale research projects sponsored by the Research Programmes Committee, Central Planning Commission, New Delhi, from 1956 to 1958. The first project in which he was involved was the '*Culture Change Evaluation Project*' conducted by the Department of Anthropology of Ranchi University during 1956-1957, and the second one was 1957-1958 the '*Rural Change Research Project*' conducted by the Institute of Social Sciences, Agra University, Agra. Thereafter he received a Pre-doctoral Fellowship from Wenner-Gren Foundation for Anthropological Research Inc., New York, in 1958, for a study on the impact of Christianity on the Uraon tribe (Oraon, now the official spelling in Census). This fellowship helped him to complete his fieldwork among the Uraons. In 1961, he joined the Postgraduate Department of Anthropology, at Ranchi University, as a Lecturer. His study on the *'Impact of Christianity on the Uraon of Three Villages in Chotanagpur'*, was the basis of his doctoral thesis which he submitted to Ranchi University in 1963. In 1964, Dr K. N. Sahay was awarded a Ph.D. degree from Ranchi University. His Ph.D. topic was '*The Impact of Christianity on the Uraon of Three Villages in Chotanagpur.*' (Unpublished Doctoral Thesis, Ranchi University, Ranchi).

In 1961, Dr Sahay joined the Postgraduate Department of Anthropology of Ranchi University as a Lecturer, and in 1970, he was made Reader in the same department. In 1981, he was elevated to the post of Professor in the same department. He was awarded a Visiting Fellowship during the years 1973-75 by the Indian Institute of Advanced Study, Simla, and at that time did his research on the '*Hindu Shrines of Chotanagpur*'. While at Agra he worked in multi-caste Hindu villages of Agra district under the '*Rural Change Research Project*' conducted by the Institute of Social Sciences, Agra University, during 1957-58. Dr K. N. Sahay was Deputy Director in the research project on '*Tribal Leadership in Bihar*', sponsored by the R.C.P., Central Planning Commission, New Delhi, (later transferred to ICSSR), and the project was conducted by the Department of Anthropology, Ranchi University. Prof. L. P. Vidyarthi and Dr K. N. Sahay later published their study on tribal leadership in 1976 (Vidyarthi and Sahay, 1976).

Dr K. N. Sahay's field of specialisation and interest included studies on culture change, religion, social structure, Indian civilisation, and tribal studies in Chotanagpur. Nine research scholars had completed their doctoral work under his supervision. All their research topics were associated with different aspects of anthropology. The research topics of some of Prof. Sahay's students are not in the conventional field of anthropology. Like the one of Dr Anil Kishore Sinha (M.Sc. in 1981), now a Professor at Panjab University, his Ph.D. thesis topic was '*Anthropology of Sweetmeats: Its Tradition and Diffusion with Special Reference to Bihar and West Bengal*', under the supervision of Prof.. K. N. Sahay. Anil Kishore Sinha was awarded a Ph.D. degree in 1986.

Dr K. N. Sahay was invited for a brief orientation course in filmmaking that was held in Tokyo in 1977. After returning from Tokyo he started bringing out a small bulletin on 'Visual Anthropology' and got it published from Ranchi. For a few years, the bulletin came out in print and some of us in the department had received complimentary copies of the first issue, but later after two or three years, I found the bulletin publication discontinued. This might have happened due to the paucity of funds for publication at that time.

Dr K. N. Sahay was Co-Chairman of the Commission on Visual Anthropology of the IUAES during 1973-78 and organised an International Symposium at the Delhi IUAES Congress that was held in 1978. Prof. Sahay organised another symposium in the year 1983 on 'Spiritual Anthropology' during the XIth International Congress of Anthropological and Ethnological Sciences (ICAES), held in Vancouver, Canada. He had intended to develop a volume on 'Spiritual Anthropology', but till the year 1986 that remained unpublished as revealed in his book (Sahay, 1986) '*Christianity and Culture Change in India*'.

The superannuation of Prof. K. N. Sahay from the University Department of Anthropology happened in the year 1995. After his retirement from the university service he got himself involved in literary work in Hindi and in Maghi language. Some of his Hindi novels are Jubeda Bai, Sapta Suran, Punarvas, and Halthin Holkhun Maghi language. His novels in Hindi and Maghi were published by Sindhu Smriti Prakashan, Ranchi. Some of his novels are still unpublished, and I have been informed that his sons are taking an interest in getting them published. His four sons are all well-established in their respective fields. Eldest son Sanjay Kumar is presently General Manager, NCL, Coal India. His second son, Rajeev Sahay is a writer, director, producer, and proprietor of a Movie Company (*Red Horse*) in Mumbai; and his fourth son, Manoj Sahay has always assisted his father in his research work at home and outside in his field studies. His third son Anjani Kumar is presently an Ambassador in Mali (West Africa).

Prof. Sahay spent some months abroad with his third son Anjani Kumar, who was in the Foreign Service of the Government of India at the time when Prof. Sahay retired. Prof. Keshari Nandan Sahay died on 18 August 2013.

The doctoral thesis of Dr K. N. Sahay submitted to Ranchi University in 1963 is an intensive and microscopic study of three Uraon villages of which one belonged to the Roman Catholic, and the other to the Lutheran denomination of Christianity. The third village consisted of a mixed population of Catholics and Lutheran Uraon converts and non-Christian Uraons. All these villages were selected from Chainpur — a very important Christian belt of Chotanagpur. In his later publication that appeared in 1976 (Sahay, 1976), *Under the Shadow of the Cross*, Dr Sahay added one more Uraon village in his study which was a predominantly non-Christian village selected from the Gumla area. Dr K. N. Sahay did his doctoral research under the supervision of Prof. L. P. Vidyarthi. Prof. L. P. Vidyarthi writes about this book in his Foreword (1976: viii-ix) '.....this study leads to discover a series of five cultural processes viz. Oscillation, Scrutinisation, Combination, Indigenisation, and Retroversion. An attempt has been made to associate these processes loosely with the beginning or later phases in the growth of Christianity.' Dr Sahay found, at the family level, Christianity has brought about a transformation in the basic concept of marriage and family life, while at the individual level; Christianity has worked as an important factor in modifying the socialisation and training process of the child and has given almost equal religious status to men and women.

Once I asked him, what is the distinctive difference between *Sarna* and Christianity? His pointed reply was: that the striking difference is — that *Sarna* is an oral tradition, while Christianity is a written tradition.

Prof. K. N. Sahay developed a small book of 90 pages on *Tribal Identity in Chotanagpur* when he was on a post-doctoral assignment under the Indian Institute of Advanced Studies, Simla, as a Visiting Fellow in 1972-73. He worked on this study when he was conducting fieldwork at Jamadohar, a Christian village in the Simdega area of Ranchi district in 1973. During his fieldwork, he came to know about the conversion from one tribal group to another and thus, the change of their identity in some villages of that area attracted his attention at that time. He discussed this aspect in his book on '*Tribal Identity*' under four sections: tradition and historical background; factors behind the change of tribal identity; procedure adopted in changing the tribal identity; and lastly cases related to the change of tribal identity. Though the historical background is controversial, however, Dr K. N. Sahay has cited some case studies where such conversions have taken place in the villages he studied. In his study of the change in tribal identity, Dr Sahay observed the change from the Kharia to the Munda group and from Uraon to the Munda community. The maximum number of cases of conversion he found related to the change of identity from the Kharia to the Munda group. The procedure of conversion, as he found (Sahay, 1986:31), is: 'Any Kharia willing to become a Munda should first find out a specific Munda clan into which he wants himself to be incorporated; or whether the people of that particular clan are ready to accept him as a member of their clan.' This conversion happened mostly among Dudh Kharias. Dr Sahay had observed that this conversion was to escape exploitation from the clutches of landlords who are Hindus, and the Mundas being a powerful community in that area can give protection to the Kharias in such a situation. So, Kharias preferred conversion to Munda under such situations. It is interesting to investigate if such situations are still prevailing in the Simdega and Kolebira regions of Jharkhand today.

Dr K. N. Sahay's interest in the study of Hindu shrines of Chotanagpur developed during 1957-58, after completing his postgraduate studies in 1956. During 1957-58 he had to tour extensively the interior villages of Chotanagpur in connection with a research assignment under the direction of Prof. Vidyarthi and he was assigned the work of an observer during the election time. During this tour of the interior rural areas of Chotanagpur, he saw some ruins of ancient shrine structures amidst tribal habitations, which surprised him at that time and aroused his curiosity and interest in the history of these ruins. In his search for religious ruins, he came to know about the ruins of Tanginath, popular as a 'picnic spot' amongst the tribals of the area. However, he got the opportunity to visit the ruins of the ancient shrine for the first time during the year 1966. That was followed by his visits to other important old shrines of Chotanagpur for a detailed study of Tanginath.

Dr Sahay confined his study of the Tanginath shrine, focusing on the involvement of the tribals in the shrine. He also did a longitudinal study of Tanginath, the ancient Hindu shrine of Chotanagpur, with emphasis on the history of the region, analyzing folklore of the area and oral traditions, temple design, and some archaeological materials related to the shrine and the area.

Dr Sahay's monograph on Tanginath (*Hindu Shrines of Chotanagpur: Case Study of Tanginath*, published in 1975) was based on his fieldwork during the years 1966 and 1967 in the village Majhgaon, situated sixteen miles west of Chainpur in the extreme western part of Ranchi district under Gumla subdivision in Dumri block. Dr Sahay visited the Tanginath shrine at the village Majhgaon for the third time in the year 1971 to conduct fieldwork with a group of postgraduate students of anthropology at Ranchi University. He did his last fieldwork in Majhgaon village for a brief period in October 1972.

Tanginath is a hill shrine in the village of Majhgaon. The area is predominantly inhabited by the Uraon Christian converts (Sahay, 1975:24). The Tanginath shrine lies on table land, atop a hillock, popularly known as Tanginath *pahar*.

Dr Sahay writes (1975: 78), 'The Tanginath shrine .....has deities of Shiva-Shakti-Surya as well as Vaishnavite cults....a number of *Shivalingas*, and images of mother goddesses, Sun god, Shiva-Parvati, Ganesh and a big iron trident ....Hanuman, Vishnu, Radha-Krishna and Balaram and others. The priests of Tanginath shrine are being assisted by some families of the Kherwar tribe. Tanginath god has a *Tangi* or axe associated with him, hence the name, which is a local deity, and his name has been used locally as a synonym for Sri Krishna Bhagawan, Prithinath, and Bholanath (Lord Shiva) who are great traditional deities. Tanginath temple is considered a Shiva temple, and the mode of worship associated with the god indicates.....that the concept of this local deity has become combined with the concept of Lord Shiva (Sahay, 1975:80).

Apart from religious studies in Chotanagpur Prof. Sahay had also done some research in Visual Anthropology, and his research articles were published in the '*Visual Anthropology Bulletin*' that he had started editing after his return from Tokyo, where he received training under an orientation course in film making by NAV.

Dr K. N. Sahay has published over fifty research articles in reputed journals in India and abroad and has authored five books independently and one book with Prof. Vidyarthi. Professor Keshari N. Sahay's work on Christianity and culture change, and the impact of Christianity on the tribes of Chotanagpur, are landmark studies. About his research in this field on Christianity in Chotanagpur, Professor S. C. Dube had commented 'an original work which breaks new ground'.

Professor Keshari Nandan Sahay died on 18 August 2013.

Some of the important publications of Prof. Keshari N. Sahay are as follows:

Sahay, Keshari N. 1975. *Hindu Shrines of Chotanagpur: Case Study of Tanginath.* Indian Institute of Advanced Study; Simla.

Sahay, Keshari N. 1976. *Under the Shadow of the Cross.* Institute of Social Research and Applied Anthropology; Calcutta.

Sahay, Keshari N. 1977. Tribal self-image and identity. In: S. C. Dube (Ed.), *Tribal Heritage in India*, Vol. I, Vikas Publishing House Pvt. Ltd.; New Delhi.

Sahay, Keshari N. 1985. *Change of Tribal Identity in Chotanagpur* (A study of conversion from one tribal group to the other). Kishore Vidya Niketan; Varanasi.

Sahay, Keshari N. 1986. *Christianity and Culture Change.* Inter-India Publications; New Delhi.

Vidyarthi, LP. and Sahay, KN 1976. *The Dynamics of Tribal Leadership in Bihar.* Kitab Mahal; Allahabad.

Chapter - 13

Prof. Aloke Kumar Ghosh: Life and Works

Sarthak Sengupta

Professor Aloke Kumar Ghosh, a renowned physical anthropologist of India was born on August 16, 1937 in Kolkata and was the only son of Late Birendra Kumar Ghosh. He was the son of a Hindu family with the practice of the Christian way of life. He remains unmarried and lived alone almost all the time of his life. He was always straightforward according to his observations, ideas, and thought.

Prof. Ghosh obtained his post-graduate degree in Anthropology from Calcutta University in 1962. Renowned anthropologists like Prof. Atul Chandra Bhowmik, Dr Gurucharan Ghosh, Prof. Rajat Kanti Das were his post-graduate batchmates. He was awarded a Ph.D. degree from the same University in 1969 under the supervision of legendary anthropologist Dr Sasanka Sekhar Sarkar. The title of his Ph.D. thesis was *'An Ethno-Biological Study of the Kota of Nilgiri Hills'*.

Prof. Ghosh served different institutions and organisations in India and abroad. He served for a brief span as a Research Officer of the Indian Council of Medical Research (August 1970 to November 1971) and the National Institute of Family Planning (November 1971 to February 1974) New Delhi. He joined the Anthropological Survey of India, Government of India as an Anthropologist (Physical) from March 1974 to July 1975. He was awarded a Post Doctoral Fellowship at John Curtin School of Medical Research in Canberra from 1975 to 1977 and worked with renowned geneticists like Prof. R.L. Kirk.

After returning home, he had to struggle all through his professional career. He served in various capacities such as Visiting Fellow of the Anthropological Survey of India (September 1979 to August 1981); Pool Officer of the Council of Scientific and Industrial Research and the Indian Statistical Institute, Kolkata. He also served as a Visiting Professor of the Department of Anthropology, at Ranchi University (1982), and Vidyasagar University. He joined the Department of Anthropology at the North Eastern Hill University (NEHU), Shillong in May 1988 as a Reader, became a Professor of Anthropology in 1993; served as Head of the Department of Anthropology, NEHU (1991-1994), and retired from the teaching service in August 1997.

Although the Department of Anthropology at North Eastern Hill University was established in 1984, however, specialised branch of Physical Anthropology was practically non-existent. Therefore, he was a real architect in building up advanced physical anthropology at NEHU, Shillong. In doing so, he envisioned integrated holistic anthropology and tried his level best to narrow down the gap between various specialised areas.

He was a member of various academic bodies like the Society for the Study of Human Biology, United Kingdom; Indian Science Congress Association, Kolkata; Indian Anthropological Society, Kolkata; Oriental Centre for Biocultural and Environmental Sciences, Kolkata; S.S. Sarkar Research Foundation for Human Sciences, Kolkata; North East India Council for Social Science Research, Shillong and many others.

Prof. Ghosh delivered a Platinum Jubilee Lecture at the 83rd Session of the Indian Science Congress Association held at Patiala, Chandigarh, Punjab in 1986 on *'β-thalassaemia: A Bio-Social Problem'* where he emphasized that an increase in genetic load is bound to increase that social load that is more amongst the poor and downtrodden of the society.

Prof. Ghosh supervised six students for their PhDs, and all of them occupied very high status in academics or administration. He supervised Ph.D. students in both physical and cultural anthropology. However, one of the following students (NM*) submitted her thesis after his superannuation:

1991. *A Bio-Social Demographic Study among the War Khasi of Meghalay.*(Romendra Khongsdier).

1993 *The Convicts of Shillong: A Socio-Demographic Study, (*Asangla Imchen Kharsling).

1996. *The Semsa: A Population Genetical Study*. (Dhruba Kumar Limbu)

1997. *A Bio-Social Study of Beta Thalassaemia,* (Mondira Bhowmik)

1998. *Khasi Cultural Resistance to Colonialism*. (Sharmila Das Talukdar)

2002. *Study on Demography and Growth Pattern among the Khasi Children of Shillong, Meghalaya* (Nandita Mukherjee)

He also mentored one M.Phil student (Ms. K. Mariamma). Apart from these, he helped a good number of Ph.D. scholars achieve their cherished goal, although they were registered students of other faculty.

Professor Ghosh contributed more than 70 research publications on his credit in different peer-reviewed journals published in India and abroad. His main thrust of the research was to screen genetic polymorphism, and rare genetic traits in numerically small reproductively isolated populations to understand the mechanism of micro-evolutionary dynamics from a bio-cultural perspective. He was also interested in the bio-cultural study of the human population and also interested in the study of family planning to understand its biological consequence by reducing the opportunity for the operation of natural selection through differential reproduction.

Professor Ghosh breathed his last on the 5th of June 2011 at Woodland Nursing Home, Kolkata after a brief illness. He decided to donate his eye and entire body after death for medical purposes.

Some selected research publications of Prof. Aloke Kumar Ghosh

Book

1973 *Physical Anthropology and its Extending Horizon.*- S.S. Sarkar Memorial Volume (Co-Editor), Orient Longman, India.

1998 *North East India: The Human Interface* (Co-Editor), Gyan Publishing House, New Delhi.

Articles

1969 ABO blood group gene frequencies in India, Pakistan, and the adjoining areas as a whole. *Man in India*. 49:372-377.

1970 Selection intensity in the Kota of Nilgiri hills, Madras, *Soc. Biol*. 17:224-225.

1972 Inbreeding in the Kota of Nilgiri hills, Madras. *Social Biology*. 19:289-291.

1973 ABO blood group and PTC taste sensitivity among the Kota of Nilgiri hills. *Hum. Hered.* 23:78-82.

1975 Some observations on the In (Indian) antigen in West Bengal (joint). *Journal of Indian Anthropological Society*, 1: 201-202.

1976 The Kota of Nilgiri hills: A demographic study. *Jr. Bio-soc Sc*.8,1:17-26.

1977 A population genetical study of the Kota in Nilgiri hills, South India, *Hum. Hered.* 27,4:225-241.

1979 Genetic load in an inbreed tribal population of South India (joint), *Hum. Genet.* 51:203-208.

1980 Haemoglobin D and E variant in Asia with special reference to India. *Journal of Indian Anthropological Society*. 15:187-206.

1991 Cultural and ecological determinants of endogamy and biological consequences, (joint). In K.N. Reddy and D.V. Raghava Rao (Eds): *Population Structure among the Tribes,* pp. 443-460, Tamil University, Ooty, Thanjavur.

1994 Bio-demographic study among the War Khasi of Meghalaya. *Journal of Indian Anthropological Society*. 29:195-202.

1996 A morpho - genetical study on the Mizo (joint). *Bulletin of the Department of Anthropology Dibrugarh University*. 24:48-62.

1996 Relevance of population study in physical anthropology, (joint), in F. A. Das and I.Barua (Eds): *Communities of North-East India,* pp. 64-74, Mittal Publications, New Delhi.

1997 Bio-anthropological profile of Meghalaya (joint), in S.Sengupta (Ed): *Studies in Anthropology: Recent Perspectives*, .pp. 170 – 200, Inter India Publications, New Delhi

1997 A genetic study on the Lyngam of Meghalaya. (joint), *Journal of Human Ecology*. 8,6: 473-475.

1997 A genetic study on the Dalu of Meghalaya. (joint), *Journal of Human Ecology*. 8,6: 477-479.

1997 A note on some morphogenetic variables among the Dalu of Meghalaya. (joint), *Journal of Human Ecology*. 8,6: 481-483.

1998 Morphological characters of foot among the Lepcha of Kalimpong, West Bengal. (joint), *Journal of Human Ecology*. 9,1: 91-93.

1998 Opportunity of selection in the Kheza of Phek district, Nagaland. (joint), *Journal of Human Ecology*. 9, 5: 515-516.

1998 Dermatoglyphics of the Lyngam of Meghalaya, India. (joint), *Journal of Human Ecology*. 9,6: 629-631.

2003 Human growth studies in North East India: A review. (joint), In M.K. Raha and A.K. Ghosh (Eds): *North East India; Human Interface*. pp. 229-250. New Delhi, Gyan Publishing House.

2004 Inbreeding in the Semsa of Semkhor village in North Cachar Hills District, Assam. (joint), *Journal of Indian Anthropological Society*.33:257-259.

2000 The Semsa: A bio-demographic study. (joint), *International Journal of Anthropology*. 15,1-2: 109-124.

Chapter - 14

Professor Atul Chandra Bhowmick: Life and Research Work

Nabakumar Duary

I

Professor Atul Chandra Bhowmick was well-known as an ideal teacher in the field of Museology. His whole life was engaged in teaching and field-based research work in the field of prehistoric culture to contemporary tribal and folk culture. He had a submissive personality and followed simple living. He honestly interacted with students and researchers and encouraged them in their research work. He remained a bachelor life and lived with the family members of his mother's sister's son at 'Uttarayan', Palta in North 24 Parganas of West Bengal. Professor Bhowmick was a thorough gentleman, with an ever-smiling face and a soft voice. He preferred wearing white trousers with a fullsleeve white shirt.

Professor Bhowmick was born on 7th January 1940 in the village of Pihar in the Comilla district of Bangladesh. He was the second child of eight offspring (Ajit, Abhilash, Basana, Mukul, Bakul, Putul, and Arun) of Akhil Chandra and Yogomaya Devi. The names of his grandparents were Mohandashi and Janakisundari. His father was one of the founding members of Deshbandhu School, Beliaghata, Kolkata, and served as a teacher in this school.

Atul Chandra studied primary education in the village school of Pihar. Then he studied at Barkanta High School in Comilla. He passed intermediate education from Maharaja Vir Vikram College,

Agartala, Tripura, and a B.Sc. in Botany, Zoology, and Anthropology from Bangabasi College, Calcutta. He obtained a Master's degree in Anthropology with specialisation in Pre-history in 1962, a Certificate of Art Appreciation in 1965, a Diploma in Museology in 1966, an M.A. in Ancient Indian History in 1969 from Calcutta University; a Ph.D. in Anthropology, from the same University in 1974 under the supervision of Professor Kalyan Gangopadhyay, Curator-in-Charge of Asutosh Museum, University of Calcutta. The title of his thesis was, '*Traditional Textiles of Bengal-A Study in Retrospect with Special Reference to Socio-economic Condition of the Weavers and Embroiderers'*. His classmates at the postgraduate level (in Anthropology) were Prof. Aloke Kumar Ghosh, Anadi Laha, Biswajit Sen, Bandana Chakraborty, Dr Gurucharan Ghosh, Narayan Bandopadhyay, Nirmalendu Dutta, Prof. Rajat Kanti Das, Samir Bose, Shyamalesh Dutta Ray and Rama Chattopadhyay. He was the recipient of the Centenary Exhibition Gold Medal of the University of Calcutta in 1974.

Atul Chandra Bhowmick served as a high school teacher in Haroa now in North 24 Parganas for a small period in 1960, then joined as Museum Caretaker of the Cultural Research Institute, Government of West Bengal from 1967 to1969; then Museum Curator, Department of Anthropology, University of Calcutta from 1972 to 1976. Later on, he joined as a Lecturer of the Museology Department at the University of Calcutta in 1976. After 29 years of teaching, he superannuated as a Professor of Museology in January 2005. He was known as a kind-hearted and honest person in his university as well as his academic circle in educational institutions and research organisations in India. He would go out of his way to help students and the staff of the University.

He specialised in Advanced Prehistoric Archaeology, with a special interest in Early Indian Pottery, Mesoliths, and Applied Archaeology. However, he was engaged in the scientific interpretation of Ethnological specimens. Bhowmick studied Palaeolithic tool-making techniques to folk technology, Palaeolithic to contemporary folk culture, folk knowledge to folk tradition, the museum to preservation, plastic art form to performing art, and statistical analysis of village survey data, etc.

He was a visiting fellow in the Department of Anthropology of Dibrugarh University and one of the founding members of the

Department of Museology, at Rabindra Bharati University. Prof. Bhowmik meticulously documented all museum objects at Rard Sanskriti Sanghralaya, Bidisa. He had vast research experience in diversified fields of different disciplines. Besides conducting research under the University Grants Commission, New Delhi, he was also awarded the Nehru Trust Research Grant in 1995-1996. Professor Bhowmick supervised 25 doctoral theses on various important topics in museology, anthropology, and folklore. His students are working in India and abroad and are in good academic positions.

Professor Atul Chandra Bhowmick wrote numerous articles on diverse topics in Anthropology, Museology, and Folklore. A variety of articles of wide range by the Professor indicates his interest in separate subjects. He published 128 articles, both in English and Bengali in reputed academic journals, magazines, and edited books. He was trained in anthropology and later turned to museology. Here are mentioned some title of the principle publications of Professor Bhowmick which were published in famous academic journals and periodicals like - *The Stone Age in West Bengal, Occurrence of Microlithic tools in Kattara site in Midnapore District, West Bengal; An Analysis of Lithic Industry of Puruliya in West Bengal; Neolithic Traits: A Global and Local Perspective; Megalithism: A Living Culture in India, Prehistoric Technology of West Bengal; Prehistoric India: Settlement Patterns; Land Utilisation and Early Subsistence, Prehistoric Art in India: A Visual Expression; Indian Pottery: Technique of Manufacture; Pottery of Khuranda Village in Monghyr; Preservation of Pottery Objects in Modern Museums; Tribal Terracotta Votive Offerings: Their Making Technique and Field Observation;The Santals of India; Marriage on Santal Community, Santal Costume; Santal Dance, A study of Mask Dance of Seraikella; Gambhira: A Mask Dace of Malda;The Hunting Tradition of Hos of Jharkhand; Ethnic Identity of the Kharnti: A Contextual Profile; A Study on Tribal Drinks, A Study of the Emerging Socio Economic Patterns of the Displaced JhaloMalos; A Brief Sketch of the Mru and Mech Tribes of West Bengal; Means of Upliftment of the Other Backward Classes; Seeing of Forest from Tribal Life;Tribal Wall Painting: A Vibrant Tradition of West Bengal; Indigenous Knowledge of Tribal Communities; Problems of Tribal Integration;Importance of Ethnographic Museum in India and Issues in Tribal Integration and the Role of Museums*, and many more.

One compiled volume entitled *Anthropological Discourses: A Collection of Essays on Culture and Heritage* was published by Professor Bhowmick in 2022 from Anustup, and foreward by his student Professor Stephen Inglis, Carleton University, Ottawa, Canada. Here he discussed from the Stone Age to the present socio-cultural scenario of tribal life with a holistic view of various anthropological issues and included detailed field studies.

Professor Bhowmick has delivered many memorial lectures on famous academicians and personalities like Professor J.K. Bose, and Professor P.K. Bhowmick in the Institute of Social Research and Applied Anthropology, Bidisa; Mahatma Gandhi in The Gandhi Smarak Sanghralaya, Barrackpore, Radharani and Annapurna on different occasions organised by respective organisations.

Professor Bhowmick was a life member of the Indian Anthropological Society, Kolkata, National Confederation and Academy of Anthropologists, Kolkata, Sasanka Sarkar Memorial Society, Kolkata, and Museum Association of India, Kolkata. He was Joint Secretary of the Museum Association of India and also a member of the development committee of the Ananda Niketan Kristhishala, Bongaon; P.C. Mahalanobis Memorial Museum and Archives of the Indian Statistical Institute, Kolkata, as an advisor of the Central Museum of Anthropological Survey of India and the Bangiyo Sahitya Parisad Museum, Kolkata. Professor Atul Chandra Bhowmick received the Lifetime Achievement Award from the Museum Association of West Bengal in 2016 and was felicitated as an ideal teacher from the University of Calcutta.

Professor Atul Chandra Bhowmick was a popular teacher not only among the students but he was also popular among the teaching and non-teaching staff of his department and other departments due to his good behaviour and polite appearance. The research area of Professor Atul Chandra Bhowmick was vast and unique. However, one of his pioneering types of research on textile design, symbols, and motives of Bengal *Sarees*.

In his old age with an acute health problem, he kept engaged in reading and writing research papers and discussing academic matters over the cell phone. Professor Bhowmick was suffering from prolonged illness due to a kidney problem and was under treatment by a specialised Doctor. Eventually cruel hand of death snatched away a charming, unique, and ideal teacher Professor Atul Chandra Bhowmick on 30th July 2023 at the age of 83 years and 6 months.

Some important publications of Professor Atul Chandra Bhowmick

1967-Museums and a neglected aspect and National integration, *Bulletin of West Bengal Head Masters Association*, Kolkata, Special Museum Issue.

1967-State ethnology, museum and the educational function, *Bulletin of Cultural Research Institute*, Vol. VI, No. 1 and 2.

1968-Museum and library in mass education, *Granthagar, Bulletin* of Bengal Library Association, Vol. 17, No. 10.

1985-Pottary of Khuranda village in Munghyr, *Folklore*, Vol. 26, No. 1.

1997-Prehistoric technology of West Bengal, In C. P. Sinha (Ed): *Art, Archaeology, and Culture of North-North-eastern India*, Puravid Parishad, Patna, Bihar.

1999-Santal dance, *Tribal Dances in India,* Edited by Robin D. Tribhuwan and Preeti R. Tribhuwan, New Delhi, Discovery Publishing House (pp. 303-305).

2010-Megalithism: A living culture of India, In B. K. Goswami (Ed): *Felicitation Volume of HK. Prasad, Journal of the Bihar Puravid Parishad,* Vols. 21-22.

2011-Lokoshilpa: Bibhinna dristikon theke, in *Lokojashilpa*, Edited by Barunkumar Chakraborty, Parul Prakashan, Kolkata (pp. 474-481, in Bengali).

2012-The indigenous art form of the Patuas of West Bengal. In D K Midya (Ed): *Indigenous People in India: Identity, Empowerment and Discontent,* APH Publishing Corporation, New Delhi (pp. 43-62).

2016-Terracotta art of Bengal, in Amitabha Sarkar, Samira Dasgupta and Nabakumar Duary (Eds): *Attributes of Culture-Reflection of Cultural Itineraries from a Multicultural Nation,* Aayu Publications, New Delhi (pp. 86-99).

2017-Kalighat paintings, *Journal of Department of Museology*, 13: 1-10.

2022-Raboti Mohan Sarkar, in Sarthak Sengupta (Ed): *Architects of Anthropology in India*, Vol. II, Gyan Publications, New Delhi, pp. 273-276.

2023-Prehistory of North-East India, In Sarthak Sengupta and Juri Borah (Eds): *Society and Culture of North East India,* Mittal Publications, New Delhi.

1411-Banglar poramatir shilpa, *Upatyaka,*Medinipur (in Bengali).

Acknowledgement

The author thanks Srimati Bratati Roy, a relative of Professor Atul Chandra Bhowmick, Dr Dipak Kumar Bara Panda, Curator, Asutosh Museum, University of Calcutta, Swarup Bhattacharya, Visiting Fellow of the Anthropological Survey of India, Kolkata and Dr Sachin Bhattacharya, Former Professor of Museology, University of Calcutta, for giving information for writing this article.

References

Anthropologists in India 1970. *Anthropologists in India*, Association Indian Anthropological Association, Delhi (pp. 9 and 85).

Bara Panda, Dipak Kumar 2021. Atulaniyo Atulchandra, *Alipore bartya,* 26 December 2020– 01 January 2021 (in Bengali).

Basu, Arabinda, Basu, MP and Adhikary Ahsim, K. 1981, *Directory of Anthropologists in India,* Anthropological Survey of India, Calcutta (pp. 43-44).

Bhowmick, Atul Chandra, 2022, *Anthropological Discourses: A Collection of Essays on Culture and Heritage,* Anustup Prakashani, Kolkata.

Indian Anthropological Association: 1978. *Anthropologists in India,* Indian Anthropological Association, Delhi (pp. 15).

Chapter - 15

Prof. Birinchi Kumar Medhi: A Beacon of Social Anthropology in North-east India

Monimugdha Bhuyan

Prologue

Professor Birinchi Kumar Medhi was a renowned social scientist in India. His extensive research encompassed multifarious dimensions of North-east India's society and culture. He was not only a distinguished anthropologist of North-east India but was well recognised as a litterateur, poet, and lyricist. He was born on November 14, 1948, in Mangaldoi town of Darrang District, Assam. His father Late Bipin Chandra Medhi was a great freedom fighter. His mother Late Snehalata Medhi was a renowned educationist. Emerging from a lineage of esteemed and erudite ancestry, Birinchi Kumar Medhi grew up with a strong foundation in good morals, ethical values, and exemplary character. He was well-acknowledged as an excellent teacher of anthropology and a proficient researcher. He garnered significant popularity among his students due to his approachable nature. Under his skillful mentorship, he nurtured and guided numerous scholars to fruition. Besides anthropological contributions, he had made remarkable contributions to Assamese literature, enriching it with a vast array of creations such as short stories, essays, riddles, and children's poems.

Education life

After completing his basic schooling in Mangaldoi, Assam, Birinchi Kumar Medhi went to Guwahati to complete his higher education. In 1964, he passed his matriculation examination from Cotton Collegiate High School of Guwahati. Then, he went to Shillong to pursue Pre-University classes. In 1965, he completed his Pre-University classes in Science from St. Anthony's College and returned to Guwahati to study Bachelor's Degree in Anthropology. He was admitted to the prestigious Cotton College of Guwahati from where he passed his B.Sc. examination in 1969 with Honours in Anthropology. He was awarded the B.S. Guha Medal for securing the first position among the Anthropology Honours students of both the Arts and Science streams. He completed his M.Sc. degree in Anthropology from Gauhati University in the year 1971. He achieved the first class - first position in Anthropology at Gauhati University that year and received a gold medal. Apart from anthropology, Birinchi Kumar Medhi was much intrigued by Assamese literature, and therefore, he again pursued a Master's degree in Assamese from Gauhati University in the year 1978. He carried out his doctoral research among the Assamese Sikhs distributed throughout the Brahmaputra Valley. As the outcome of his rigorous research, he submitted his thesis entitled, *The Assamese Sikhs: A Study on their Social Relations in a Rural Context of Assam,* which was done under the able guidance of Prof. A.N.M. Irshad Ali. For his phenomenal research, Birinchi Kumar Medhi was awarded the Ph.D. degree in Anthropology by Gauhati University in 1990.

Service life

Dr Birinchi Kumar Medhi started his academic career as a Lecturer of Anthropology at Arya Vidyapeeth College, Guwahati. He joined the college on November 27, 1972, and continued teaching there till March 24, 1981. He joined the Department of Anthropology, Gauhati University, as a Lecturer on March 25, 1981. Dr Medhi was promoted to Reader in Anthropology on October 24, 1991. On December 1, 1999, he became a Professor of Anthropology at Gauhati University. Professor Medhi acted as the Head of the Department from 2003 to 2006. He retired from his service at Gauhati University on October 31, 2013. He had organised and participated in numerous Seminars, Conferences, and Workshops both in India and abroad. Among them, mention may be made of a National Seminar organised by Professor Medhi along with Indira Gandhi Rashtriya Manav Sangrahalaya, Bhopal was on *'Intangible Cultural Heritage of Assam'*, held on

September 28-30, 2006 in collaboration with Gauhati University and Srimanta Sankardev Kalakshetra, Guwahati. He possessed excellent skills as an ethnographer and had taken many batches of students for ethnographic fieldwork.

Throughout his lifetime, he had efficaciously mentored thirty-three numbers of Ph.D. research scholars from different Universities such as Gauhati University, Krishna Kanta Handiqui State Open University, and Assam Don Bosco University. Professor Medhi was very particular in choosing the topic of research of his scholars. The domain of research of his scholars covers a wide range of thought-provoking and captivating topics like the study of aged in old age homes, orphans, disabled, alcoholism, women and child welfare, ethnomedicine, religion, enculturation, customary law, cultural tourism, silk production, mobile theatre, mask making, bamboo culture and rice culture. Moreover, the selection of the population for research was distinctive and encompassed different lesser-explored ethnic groups such as the Tagins, Miniyongs, Monpas, Hmars, Dimasas, Mahalias, Tiwas, Pati Rabhas, and the Assamese Hindus.

List of doctoral students and their studies

1998 *A Study of the Role of Voluntary Organisation for Woman's Education and Welfare in Kamrup District of Assam* (Jointly guided with Prof. Nandita Sharma). Anju Bhatia.

2004 *Child Rearing Practices in Three Tribal Societies of Assam: A Study among the Deoris, Garos and the Karbis.* Minaxi Regon.

2004 *A Study on Disease and Treatment among the Tagins of Arunachal Pradesh.* Bhabatosh Paul.

2004 *Role of Voluntary Organisations in Child Welfare in Kamrup Districts of Assam.* Dip Kr. Saikia.

2004 *Megaliths and their Associated Remains in Dimoria Area of Kamrup District, Assam.* Kalpana Chaudhury.

2008 *Socio-cultural Dimensions of the Rural Assamese Migrants in Petty Salaried Jobs in Guwahati, Assam.*Mrinal Sharmah.

2009 *Ethno-medicine among the Garos of North East India: Aspects of Traditional and Modern Health Care Practices in two Village Settings.* Rameeza Hasan.

2010 *An Anthropological Study on Mask of Natun Chamaguri Satra of Majuli, District Jorhat, Assam.* Arifur Zaman.

2010 *Changing Aspects of Religion in Plains Tribal Community of Assam: The Case of the Pati Rabhas.* Monmee Sonowal.

2010 *Traditional Health Care Practices of the Monpas of Tawang, Arunachal Pradesh.* Daisy Baishya.

2010 *An Anthropological Study of the Disable in Guwahati.* Aref Zaman.

2011 *Customary Laws among the Tiwas of Assam.* Indrani Barpujari.

2011 *Woman and Endi Silk Production in a Village of Kamrup District, Assam.* Farzana Begum.

2012 *Prospects of Sustainable Development of Cultural Tourism in South Eastern Brahmaputra Valley of Assam: An Anthropological Perspective.* Nilofar Jasmin.

2013 *A Study on Family Planning Practices in a Multi-Ethnic Setting in Goalpara District, Assam.* Monoj Gogoi.

2014 *Reproductive Health Status of the Karbi Woman in Guwahati City.* Mousumi Nath.

2016 *A Study on Festivals of Assam and France with Particular Reference to Bihu and Christmas* (Jointly guided with Prof. Gulab Jha). Bhaswati Chakrabarty.

2016 *Role of Voluntary Organisation in Women's Welfare in Kohima District, Nagaland.* Bimla.

2016 *Role of Khasi Women in Family Management and its Depiction in Khasi Folk Narratives.* Jaya Das.

2016 *An Exploration of the Aged Persons in Old Age Homes of Assam.* Mridusmita Kashyap.

2016 *An Exploration of Sukreswara and Umananda Temple in Guwahati.* Himarjyoti Talukdar.

2017 *An Anthropological Study of Orphans Living in Guwahati.* Kunal Choudhury.

2018 *An Anthropological Study of Alcoholics of Guwahati.* Hemanta Sharma.

2018 *Traditional Healing Practices among the Mahalias of Darrang District, Assam.* Chandrani Sarma.

2018 *Aspects of Donyipolo among the Miniyongs of Arunachal Pradesh.* Nirupoma Kardong.

2018 *Dimensions of Mobile Theatre of Assam* (Jointly guided with Dr Mrinal Jyoti Goswami). Sangeeta Kakoty.

2019 *Universe of Religion among the Dimasa of Assam and Nagaland with special emphasis on the Daikho System of Worship.* Humi Thaosen.

2019 *Women Depicted in Folklore: The Case of the Garos of Assam and Meghalaya with Special Reference to their Maxims and Folktales.* Sagarika Mahanta.

2019 *Dr Bhupen Hazarika's Song as Classic Prototype for Mass Communication.* Bhaskarjyoti Gogoi.

2019 *Christianity and Culture Change: An Anthropological Insight into the Hmars of Dima Hasao District, Assam.* Arindita Goswami.

2019 *Dimensions of Bamboo among the Assamese Caste People of Kamrup (Rural) District, Assam.* Jilmil Bora.

2019 *Role of Enculturation on Academic Performance of the Girl Student of Secondary Stage: The Case of the Pati Rabha of Rampur and Rani Area of Kamrup District, Assam.* Binita Baishya.

2021 *Rice Culture among the Assamese Hindus in a Rural Context of Assam: An Anthropological Insight.* Monimugdha Bhuyan.

Anthropological contributions

Birinchi Kumar Medhi started his Anthropological research among the Assamese Sikhs of Assam. He was the first person to systematically study the Assamese Sikh population for his doctoral research. From 1984 to 1987 he conducted extensive fieldwork among the Assamese Sikh inhabitants primarily of Barkola village of Nagaon District, Assam. He had further extended his research beyond Barkola village to collect data on the Assamese Sikhs residing in other parts of Assam. After completing his Ph.D., he expanded his field of research to different tribes and communities in North-east India. Special mention may be made of the Pati Rabhas, a sub-tribe of the Rabhas, whom he had thoroughly studied and contributed many noteworthy publications including their beliefs in the supernatural world, benevolent and malevolent spirits, tutelary god '*Langa*', and snake goddess '*Marai*'. He had conducted a significant number of works on ethnomedicine of different communities of Assam. Some other key areas of his research include religion, material culture, man-plant relationship, child-rearing practices, kinship, customary law, intangible culture, food habits, mask-making, rice culture, and bamboo culture.

Professor Birinchi Kumar Medhi edited many noteworthy books on Anthropology, including *Intangible Cultural Heritage of Assam* (2008, with K.K. Basa), *Tribal Development of Tripura* (2008, with G.K. Bera, R.P. Athparia and K. Jose), *Tribes of North East India: Issues and Challenges* (2009, with R.P. Athparia and K. Jose), *Social Unrest and Peace Initiatives: Perspectives from North East India* (2011, with G.K. Bera, R.P. Athparia and K. Jose) and *Concept of God and Religion: Traditional Thought and Contemporary Society* (2012, with G.K. Bera, R.P. Athparia and K. Jose). For the benefit of Assamese medium students, Prof. Medhi had penned down a few notable books of Anthropology in the Assamese language, including *Nrigosthitattwar Ruprekha* (1980, book on ethnography), *Samajik Nritattwa Sambhed* (1982, book on Social Anthropology written with A.N.M. Irshad Ali) and *Akhan Desh Alekh Manuh* (1970, appraisal of 25 tribes of India with a long poem on evolution of man). He received a Certificate of Merit from the Honourable President of India for his book *Akhan Desh Alekh Manuh* in the competition organised by NCERT for the Neo-literates. He edited two volumes of the Higher Secondary level textbook *Nritattwa Sopan* - Part I (1996) and *Nritattwa Sopan* - Part II (2004), for the Assam Higher Secondary Education Council, Guwahati. Professor Medhi has contributed more than two hundred research papers in different books and journals of National and International repute.

Literary contributions

In addition to his expertise in Anthropology, Professor Birinchi Kumar Medhi was acclaimed as a distinguished literary luminary of Assam who had contributed tremendous treasure to Assamese literature. He had penned down many intriguing short stories, essays, riddles, and poems for children. He was also a frequent contributor of different articles, poems and short stories to the newspapers and magazines of Assam. He used to write songs, dramas, scripts, and documentaries for Gauhati Radio Centre, Guwahati Doordarshan Kendra, and many other organisations.

Publications on child literature

1968 *Antareep* (children's short story), Guwahati, New Book Stall.

1979 *Amar Prativeshi Patanga* (essays on common insects for children), Guwahati, Barua Agency.

1979 *Ag Chotalar Mel* (riddles and poems for children), Guwahati, L.B. S. Publications.

1980 *Akhan Desh Alekh Manuh* (appraisal of 25 tribes of India with a long poem on evolution of man), Mangaldai, Chakrabarty Brothers.

1981 *Ateejar Sadhu* (stories for children from scriptures), Guwahati, Radha Prakashan.

1982 *Abhinandita Avasad* (short stories), Nalbari, Journal Emporium.

1984 *Akash Jiman* (short stories), Guwahati, Barua Agency.

1985 *Ajanmar Sahachar* (novel), Guwahati, Mani Manik Prakash.

1987 *Ajari Parar Kabita* (poems for children), Guwahati, Radha Prakashan.

1993 *Asamiya Upanyas Sahityar Niryas* (edited articles on Assamese novels), Guwahati, Golok Roymedhi Smriti Prakashan.

1998 *Charachar* (essays), Nalbari, Journal Emporium.

1998 *Podum Patar Pani* (essays), Guwahati, Sabinary.

1998 *Lokaranya* (essays), Guwahati, Mani Manik Prakash.

1999 *Akular Kabita* (poems for children), Guwahati, Radha Prakashan.

2007 *Ankurar Para Aranyaloi* (children's book on plants and forest), Guwahati, Asam Prakashan Parisad.

Professor Birinchi Kumar Medhi was endowed with excellent skills in anthem composition. He had crafted anthems for various institutions and organisations, including Arya Vidyapeeth College, Krishna Kanta Handiqui State Open University, K. C. Das Commerce

College, J. B. Law College, West Guwahati Commerce College, South Guwahati Junior College, Dudhnoi College, Puthimari College, Pub Kamrup College, Bejera Anchalik College, Vidya Bharati College, Surashree Sangeet Mahavidyalaya, Assam Kick-Boxing Association, Gauhati Sports Association, Balichandra Club, Sangeet Kanan Music College, Anthropological Society of North East India, and Eastern India Woman Association. In addition to anthem composition, he possessed mastery in composing lyrics. He composed lyrics for many evergreen melodies of Assam. His talent as a lyricist was acknowledged by the Government of Assam as he was bestowed with the Best Lyricist award twice at the Assam State Film Awards in 2010 and 2015.

Academic associations

During his service life and even after his retirement, Professor Birinchi Kumar Medhi was actively associated with several academic bodies and institutions. He served as a member of the Court of Assam University, a member of graduate and postgraduate boards of different Universities, and a member of the Governing body of multiple colleges. He was a founder member of different bodies like the Indian National Confederation and Academy of Anthropologists (INCAA), Sanskriti - North Eastern Institute of Culture and Religion, and a Life Member of the North East Council for Social Science Research, Anthropological Society of North East India, and Assam Sahitya Sabha. He also acted as the Vice-President of the Dr Bhupen Hazarika Foundation (BHF) since its inception. Professor Medhi had an amiable relationship with many Anthropology Departments in the country. As a resource person for seminars and conferences, invited speaker, interviewer, paper setter, and moderator, and also as an external examiner of Doctoral and Postgraduate examinations, he had visited a good number of academic institutions in the country. He was a frequent visitor to North Bengal University, Visva-Bharati University, Assam University, Dibrugarh University, and Cotton University for various academic pursuits even in the later part of his life. He was often invited to different colleges of Assam for academic as well as non-academic assignments. In 2012, KIIT and KISS University in Bhubaneswar honoured Professor Birinchi Kumar Medhi with the title of 'Living Anthropologist' in recognition of his ceaseless academic contributions to the field of Anthropology.

Conclusion

The health condition of Prof. Birinchi Kumar Medhi started deteriorating abruptly in the later months of 2022. His condition worsened in the starting days of 2023 and was hospitalised for more than a month in Guwahati. Professor Medhi left for his heavenly abode on February 22, 2023, at the age of 74 years at Assam Down Town Hospitals, Guwahati. His demise created a void in the Indian Anthropology community, particularly in Assam and North-east India. Throughout his life, he went above and beyond to connect with his students and create a welcoming and supportive learning environment. He was known for his kindness, empathy, and patience for which his students felt comfortable sharing their struggles and success with him. He was not just a teacher but also a mentor, guide, and friend to many of his students who always lent an ear and offered advice when needed. Not only his students but people from different sections of society had a cordial rapport with him. His ability to connect with people from all walks of life was truly remarkable. Being his final Ph.D. student, the author expresses his irredeemable indebtedness and gratitude to Professor Birinchi Kumar Medhi for his erudition, priceless counsel, scholarly inputs, and consistent encouragement not only in his research but also in every facet of life.

Selected publications of Prof. Birinchi Kumar Medhi

1980 Dress habit of the Adis of Arunachal, *Journal of the Assam Science Society,* 23: 64 - 68.

1980 Beliefs, events of rituals and ceremonies connected with the principal the life of the Pati Rabhas of Assam, *Bulletin of the Department of Anthropology,* Dibrugarh University, IX: 40-53.

1981 Cultural spectrum of the Phakes: Material Culture, *Journal of the Assam Science Society*, 24,1. 33-37.

1982 Some aspects of beliefs in the Pati Rabha society, *Gauhati University Journal of Science*, 28: 6 -12.

1983 Langa - the tutelary God of the Pati Rabhas of Assam, *Journal of the North East India Council for Social Science Research,* 7,1: 31-33.

1984 Snake Goddess Marai of the Pati Rabhas of Assam, *The Eastern Anthropologist,* 37,2: 159-166.

1985 Concept of supernatural among the Pati Rabhas of Assam, *Journal of the North East India Council for Social Science Research*, 9,1: 41-43.

1986 A few female malevolent spirits of the Pati Rabhas of Assam, *Journal of the North East India Council for Social Science Research*, 10,1: 53-56.

1987 Man-plant relationship in a heterogeneous village: A case study, *Journal of the Assam Science Society*, 29,4: 20-27.

1988 The Karbi society at a glance, *Souvenir: Anthropological Society of North East India,* XXXIII Annual Session (1987 – 1988): 8-13.

1990 Marriage among the Rangdani Rabhas of Assam: An appraisal (with Mrinal Sharma), *Journal of the North East India Council for Social Science Research,* 14,1: 64-67.

1991 Glimpses of village and house type of the Karbis, *Journal of North East Indian Council for Social Science Research,* 14,2: 8-10.

1993 *The Assamese Sikhs: Profile of a minuscule community* (with A.N.M. Irshad Ali), In S.B. Roy and A.K. Ghosh (Eds.): *People of India,* Delhi, Inter India Publication: pp. 277-287.

1994 Economy of the Karbis, In Sarthak Sengupta (Ed.): *Tribes of North East India*, New Delhi, Gyan Publishing House: pp. 127-133.

1995 Ethno-medicine: A study among the Mishings in a rural context of Assam, *Bulletin of the Department of Anthropology*, Gauhati University, IX: 61-68.

2001 Child-rearing practices among the Plain dwelling Garos of Goalpara District, Assam (with Queenbala Marak), *Man and Life,* 27,3 & 4: 213-222.

2003 Some observations on the Hiras in a rural context of Lower Assam (with Arifur Zaman), *Arunachal University Research Journal.* 6,1: 111-117.

2003 Causes and diagnosis of ailments and diseases among the Garos of Assam (with Rameeza Hasan), *Journal of the North East India Council for Social Science Research*, 27,2: 38-45.

2004 Mask makers of a Vaishnavite monastery of Assam (with Arifur Zaman), *Journal of North East India Council for Social Science Research,* 28,1: 4-8.

2004 Health and hygiene of the Nahs of Arunachal Pradesh (with Bhabatosh Paul), *Studies of Tribes and Tribals*, 2,1: 23-27.

2005 Some selected motifs of *Gamocha* from Assam and their meanings (with Sankar Kr. Roy), *Humankind - Journal of Indira Gandhi Rashtriya Manav Sangrahalaya, Bhopal,* 118-130.

2006 Role of the Bansphor Caste Panchayat in a slum of Guwahati (with Indrani Barpujari), *Bulletin of the Department of Anthropology,* Dibrugarh University, 34: 27-40.

2007 Use of ethnomedicinal plants among the Lalungs in a rural context of Assam (with Aref Zaman), *Bulletin of the Department of Anthropology*, Dibrugarh University, 35: 39-50.

2008 Tribal development in Assam, people's participation, NGO's and Government (with K. Jose), In Girindra Nath Das (Ed.): *Tribal Development in North East India*, Guwahati, Director, Assam Institute of Research for Tribals and Schedule Castes: 17-32.

2008 Jonbeel Mela: A catalyst fair for peace and amity (with Arifur Zaman), In Girindra Nath Das (Ed.): *Tribal Development in North East India,* Guwahati, Director, Assam Institute of Research for Tribals and Schedule Castes: pp. 267-274.

2008 Tradition of mask at a Vaishnavite monastery of Assam (with Arifur Zaman), In Kishor K. Basa and Birinchi K. Medhi (Eds.): *Intangible Cultural Heritage of Assam*, Delhi, Pratibha Prakashan: 213-224.

2009 Concept of Jagannatha among the Assamese Hindus, In R. N. Dash (Ed.): *Jagannatha in Historical Perspectives*, Bhopal, Indira Gandhi Rashtriya Manav Sangrahalaya: 77-89.

2009 Tradition of utensils, In Basanta Deka (Ed.): *Assam: Land and People*, New Delhi, Thomson Press (India) Ltd.: pp. 169-173.

2010 Glimpses of modernisation among the Kaibartas of Boripara, Assam (with Chandana Sharma), In Jayanta Borborah, and

Vinay Kr. Srivastava (Eds.): *Issues in Contemporary Society*, Guwahati, DVS Publishers: 70-78.

2011 Aspects of orphans in Guwahati City (with Kunal Choudhury), In G. K. Bera and K. Jose (Eds.): *Anthropological Researches in India: Retrospect and Prospect,* Mittal Publication, India: pp. 56-63.

2012 Age at marriage and fertility behaviour: An exploration among the Muslim women in rural areas of Assam (with Monoj Gogoi), *Nrtattv – Journal of the Department of Anthropology*, Visva – Bharati, 2, 2: 5-18.

2013 Aspects of blinds in an organisational setting of Guwahati (with Aref Zaman), *Nrtattv – Journal of the Department of Anthropology*, Visva – Bharati, 3: 15-27.

2014 Spectrum of the Sikpui – Ruoi festival of the Hmar tribe of Assam (with Arindita Goswami), *Nrtattv – Journal of the Department of Anthropology*, Visva – Bharati, 4,6: 1-12.

2014 Preservation of plants among the Assamese Hindus through pristine religious system (with Dhanmani Medhi), In Pradip Sharma, Santanu Phukan, Gautam Mazumdar, and Churamoni Saikia (Eds.): *Eco-restoration for Development in India's North East*, Visakhapatnam, Global Publishing House: pp. 154-162.

2014 Dimensions of clan and descent: The case of the Dimasas of Assam (with Humi Thaosen), *Bulletin of the Department of Anthropology*, Dibrugarh University, 42: 21-36.

2015 Advent of Vaishnavism in an animistic enviorn: The case of the Deoris of Assam (with Monimugdha Bhuyan), *North Bengal Anthropologist*, 3: 17-26.

2016 Bamboo culture in Assam: Its reflection in day-to-day Assamese language (with Jilmil Bora), *Nrtattv – Journal of the Department of Anthropology*, Visva – Bharati , 9,10: 11-24.

2017 Aspects of rice culture among the Assamese Hindus in two rural contexts of Assam (with Monimugdha Bhuyan), In R. R. Das (Ed.): *Folklore in North East India: Continuity and Change,* New Delhi, Lakshmi Publishers and Distributors: pp. 57-80.

2017 Language of the Assamese utensils, In R. Khongsdier and Sarthak Sengupta (Eds.): *People of North East India: Bio-Cultural Dimensions*, Delhi, Kalpaz Publications: pp. 235-248.

2018 Aurora of Donyipolo among the Miniyongs of Arunachal Pradesh (with Nirupoma Kardong), *Journal of North East Region, Bodoland University*, 6,3: 176-184.

2018 Grandeur of a mortuary rite: The Chomangkan of the Karbis of Assam (with Bimla), *The Asian Man*, 12,2: 173-181.

2020 Grandeur of food in an Assamese Hindu village (with Monimugdha Bhuyan), *Men Environment and Society*, 1,1: 57-68.

References

Bhuyan, Monimugdha. 2022. *Birinchi Kumar Medhi* (Obituary). *Bulletin of the Department of Anthropology, Dibrugarh University*. 50: 200-202.

Medhi, Birinchi K. 1979. *Nrigosthitattwar Ruprekha* (a book on ethnography), Guwahati, Gauhati University Coordination Committee for Production of Text Books in the Regional Languages.

Medhi, Birinchi K. 1982. *Akhan Desh Alekh Manuh,* Mangaldai, Chakraborty Brothers.

Medhi, Birinchi K. 1989. *The Assamese Sikhs: A Study on their Social Relations in a Rural Situation.* Unpublished Ph.D. Thesis, Department of Anthropology, Gauhati University, Guwahati, Assam.

Medhi, Birinchi K. and ANM. Irshad Ali, 1982, *Samajik Nritattwa Sambhed* (book on Social Anthropology, Guwahati, Gauhati University Coordination Committee for Production of Text Books in the Regional Languages.

Medhi, Birinchi K. and KK. Basa. 2008. *Intangible Cultural Heritage of Assam,* New Delhi, Pratibha Prakashan.

Medhi, Birinchi K., GK. Bera, RP. Athparia and K. Jose, 2008. *Tribal Development in Tripura*, Guwahati, EBH Publishers.

Medhi, Birinchi K., RP. Athparia and K. Jose 2009. *Tribes of North East India: Issues and Challenges,* New Delhi, Omson Publications.

Medhi, Birinchi K., GK. Bera, RP. Athparia and K. Jose. 2011. *Social Unrest and Peace Initiatives: Perspectives from North East India,* Guwahati, EBH Publishers.

Medhi, Birinchi K., GK. Bera, RP. Athparia and K. Jose, 2012. *Concept of God and Religion: Traditional Thought and Contemporary Society,* Guwahati, Abhijeet Publications.

Chapter - 16

Professor Jaydip Sen: A Versatile Anthropologist

Gopal Chandra Mandal and Arpita Mandal (Nandi)

Jaydip Sen, Jojo to us, was born on 12th December 1965, in Agartala, Tripura. He was the only child of his parents. He completed his schooling up to Higher Secondary from Shillong, Meghalaya, and was admitted to Sree Chaitanya College, Habra, North 24 Parganas, West Bengal for a graduation degree. After that, he completed his Postgraduation from the Department of Anthropology, University of Calcutta, Kolkata in 1991, specialising in Physical Anthropology and Human Genetics. During his postgraduate studies, he was interested in doing research in microelements and worked on trace elements level from hair samples in the dissertation paper. He was also interested in working on groundwater arsenic contamination.

He qualified in the UGC-NET examination and received a Junior and Senior Research Fellowship for his Doctoral degree on a topic entitled, '*Determination of essential and toxic trace element concentrations in scalp hair of the Bengalee population of West Bengal*' and was awarded Ph. D. degree from the University of Calcutta in the year 1998. Before completing his Ph. D. work in August 1996, he joined as a Lecturer in the Department of Anthropology, Bangabasi College, Kolkata. In August 2005, he joined as Reader, in the Department of Anthropology, University of North Bengal, Darjeeling, West Bengal. He became a Professor in Anthropology in the year 2008.

During his tenure at Bangabasi College, he received funding in the form of a Minor Research Project (MRP, 2003-2004) from the University Grant Commission (UGC) and worked on the '*Effect of ground-water arsenic contamination on reproductive performance of the affected individuals and their socio-economic status*'. Furthermore, he also completed another project on '*Assessment of nutritional status using anthropometric measurements and determination of trace elements in selected body tissues*' and received financial support (2008) from UGC during his tenure at North Bengal University.

He worked in collaboration with the Department of Anthropology, Punjab University, Chandigarh; the Department of Forensic Medicine, Manipal University, Mangalore and the Department of Physiology, North Bengal Medical College and Hospital, West Bengal. He also acted as a visiting faculty (UGC-Merged scheme), at the Department of Anthropology, Vidyasagar University, and from 2013, he was the editor of the journal named '*South Asian Anthropologist*', published by Serial Publication, New Delhi, India, and also was one of the members of the editorial board of several journals. During his tenure at the Department of Anthropology, University of North Bengal, he supervised Ph.D. scholars like Dr Nitish Mondal, Dr Sampreeti Debnath, Dr Pushpa Lata Tigga, and Dr Binu Dorjee.

In his earlier days as a research fellow, he was keen to research the effects of trace elements on human scalp hair and completed his Ph.D. degree under the supervision of Prof. A. B. Das Chaudhuri, Department of Anthropology, University of Calcutta. Back then in the 1990s, no one could dreamt of such work as the laboratory required for such investigations was not set up, especially in the Department of Anthropology. Jaydip had to take the help of the FUME Chamber of the Department of Agriculture on the same floor to clean and extract the trace elements from the human scalp hair. After that, he used to take the help of 'The Instrumentation Center' at Rajabazar Science College, to estimate the concentration level of trace elements like copper and lead. That was a huge task from collecting scalp hair from different occupational groups to estimation of concentration levels. At that time, the use of computer analysis was not so accessible. But Jaydip did his work with determination and dedication and published several articles in various National and International Journals. In 1995, he wrote on trace element analysis of human hair in Physical Anthropology (Sen and Das Chaudhuri, 1995a and 1995b). Then, he published on the human scalp hair as an indicator of environmental lead pollution and lead exposure (Sen, 1996; Sen and Das Chaudhuri, 1996; Sen, 1998; Sen, 2009, 2010). He also tried to evaluate the relationship between human hair diameter and medulla with their copper and lead concentrations (Sen and Das Chaudhuri, 1997). Jaydip inspired my co-author's dissertation work during her master's in Anthropology. He encouraged her to take up work on trace elements in blood, in Non-Insulin Dependent Diabetes Mellitus (NIDDM) patients (Nandi and Das Chaudhuri, 1998). Prof. Sen introduced her to the people at the Instrumentation Center, helped her out, and taught how to work in the Fume Chamber. He was very happy to see her first publication on this topic. Later, we often shared that we weren't fortunate enough to be able to continue further with works on trace or microelements.

As we go through the research publication of Prof. Sen, a change in areas of research comes up. He had been doing much work on 'trace elements' in continuation with his Ph.D. thesis, since 1995. In 2008, he published his work in *South Asian Anthropologist* entitled, 'Contributions of biological anthropologists in assessing human exposure to toxic elements with special reference to India' (Sen, 2008). He also published another article in the same year (2008) along with his supervisor, Dr Das Chaudhuri, '*Arsenic exposure through drinking water and its effect on pregnancy outcome in Bengali women*' in *Arhiv za higijenu rada I toksikologiju* (Sen and Das Chaudhuri, 2008).

As he joined the University of North Bengal in August 2005, his areas of research made a major change. This we see mostly because of the lack of laboratory, infrastructure required for the analytical part of studies related to trace elements. Moreover, there was less pollution in the new place of his work.

Prof. Sen looks for some interesting works in anthropometry, from 2007 - 2008. His works then were on the socio-economic factors affecting anthropometric measurements and indices (Tigga et al., 2015; Debnath et al., 2018a). Anthropometry and nutrition dominated his world of research although out till the end at the University of North Bengal. Right from the estimation of stature from different measurements of the body parts including digits as well, to the prevalence of malnutrition of the indigenous population of North Bengal, Prof. Sen went on with his interests in unfurling the facts lesser known to Anthropologists. These studies made him communicate with renowned Biological Anthropologists outside India, among them most eminent being, Prof. Barry Bogin, Prof. Michael Hermanussen, Prof. P. D. Christiansen Schefeller, and others.

Going through the works on anthropometry, his studies for over two decades can be sectioned into three major areas; (a) Anthropometry and nutrition, (b) Anthropometry and population variation, and (c) Anthropometry and forensic science. One of his interesting articles is on the *Prevalence of the double burden of malnutrition among Indian children* (Debnath et al., 2018b). Besides, he also reviewed the double burden situation among Indian adolescents (Debnath et al., 2019). Prof. Sen was also working on the socio-economic and demographic correlates for undernutrition, especially in the indigenous population Rajbangshis of North Bengal (Bose et al., 2020) and overweight and obesity among the Karbi women of Assam, another state of eastern India (Mondal et al., 2017a). In this article, Sen discusses how both forms of malnutrition i.e., undernutrition and overnutrition co-exist in the ommunity.

Sen set his foot in anthropometry with an assessment of nutritional status in children. He started with the help of three conventional methods of assessing undernutrition i.e., stunting, underweight, and wasting among the Rajbangshis, tea garden labourer, and Benglee Muslim children aged 5-12 years (Mondal and Sen, 2010a), among the rural adolescents from Darjeeling district (Mondal and Sen, 2012), and the Limboo children of Sikkim, India (Dorjee et al., 2020).

Side by side with the conventional methods, Prof. Sen used other measures of assessing undernutrition like thinness (low BMI for age), Mid Upper Arm Circumference (MUAC), as well as neck (Roy et al., 2021), and head circumferences (Tigga et al., 2016a). He not only tried to find out the prevalence of thinness among the rural children of West Bengal (Debnath et al., 2018c) but also among the Indian children as a whole (Mondal and Sen, 2010b). Furthermore, he also worked among the rural adolescents of North Bengal and tried to find the prevalence of stunting and thinness simultaneously (Mondal and Sen, 2010c). As we all know MUAC is an easily accessible and easily measurable anthropometric variable to estimate the level of undernutrition among children (Mondal and Sen, 2009a). Prof. Sen also used MUAC cut-off for his research (Sen et al., 2010), the important aspect is that he used MUAC – for – height as indicators of body composition and nutritional status among children (Debnath et al., 2017). On the other hand, Sen utilised neck circumference as a screening measure of overweight/ obesity among Indian adults (Mondal et al., 2016), a less used tool, and also tried to estimate the cut-off points of neck circumference to determine overweight / obesity among Asian Indian adults (Mondal et al., 2017b). He also initiated the assessment of the nutritional status of children aged 5–12 years using upper arm composition among the Bengalee Muslim population of West Bengal (Sen et al., 2011a). Effects of various socioeconomic, socio-demographic, as well as lifestyle factors on undernutrition, were also studied (Tigga et al., 2015a; 2015b) and on overweight and obesity (Rengma et al., 2015; Sinha et al., 2018). Prof. Sen also reviewed the work done on the use of BMI as an indicator of assessing the prevalence of undernutrition in India (Mondal and Sen, 2009b). In another study, Sen used mid-upper arm circumference and arm-to-height ratio as tools to estimate overweight and obesity among girls aged 5-14 years of the Bengalee Hindu caste population of Siliguri Sub-division, Darjeeling district (Roy and Sen, 2020).

He also worked on the assessment of body composition based on fat mass, percentage body fat, fat-free mass, etc. (Sen and Mondal, 2013; Debnath et al., 2018d) and he tried to evaluate the age and sex-specific variations in body composition of adults of Rajbangshi population of Darjeeling district (Roy et al., 2020). He showed the way, how to predict the body composition and nutritional status of adolescent boys by the use of upper arm composition (Sen et al., 2015a).

In his two decades of research, Prof. Sen has also been interested in population variation studies through anthropometry (Sen et al., 2011b; 2013; 2014; Mondal and Sen, 2014; Tigga et al., 2016b; Mondal et al., 2017c; Sinha et al., 2018; Roy et al., 2020). The association of maternal nutritional status with birth weight in children was a work that was much cited and discussed (Sen et al., 2010). As Sen worked in the communities both indigenous and urban in the Northern parts of Bengal, this contributed much to the other comparative studies that followed. Earlier to this, we did not have much to refer to from the North Bengal population, especially the Rajbangshi community. Prof. Sen's work on body composition will also be mentioned here like, age and sex-specific variations among Rajbangshi adults from Darjeeling district (Roy et al., 2020) and also among the rural preschool children (Debnath et al., 2018). Variation of obesity and blood pressure was another topic of research (Sarkar et al., 2009).

Prof. Sen had been always interested in the Forensic part of Anthropology. We remember our discussions way back in the 1990s while pursuing our Doctoral degree together in the same laboratory under the supervision of Prof. A.B. Das Chaudhuri. In our discussions or '*Addas*', Sen used to sadly say that, not much has been contributed from Anthropology into Forensic Science in India. Later, we find his work and publishing in this area, with a discussion on the determination of sex from the dimensions of the foot (Sen et al., 2011c). We remember him saying that this was just a little step that he had taken to look into Forensic Anthropology. Then he started working on the various aspects of dermatoglyphics (Sen et al., 2011d, Dorjee et al., 2015; Debnath and Sen, 2020). In the article (Krishan et al., 2010) Sen, includes dermatoglyphics to study sex differences, another step forward toward Forensic Anthropology. He also took the initiative to study the estimation of stature from arm span, arm length, tibial length (Dorjee and Sen, 2016); foot length, and foot breadth (Sen and Ghosh, 2008) among the Rajbangshi population and from the length of index and ring fingers (Sen et al., 2014). Not only that, but he also focused on the estimation of stature from the hand dimension (Roy et al., 2020b). Besides, he took the initiative to identify the sex from index and ring finger lengths in an indigenous population of Eastern India (Sen et al., 2015b). Along with the dermatoglyphics and anthropometric measurements in forensic anthropology, he started working on hair diameter and medulla formation among the Rajbangshis of North Bengal (Sen and Mondal, 2012).

His interest in work also spread to menopausal health among Rajbangshi women (Sinha and Sen, 2017). This was one of the pioneering works on menopausal health in a rural area in North Bengal and the first among the Rajbangshis, an indigenous community. He also tried to find out the association between age at menarche and age at menopause among women of an indigenous population of North Bengal, India (Sinha et al., 2021). He took the initiative to investigate the effect of arsenic exposure on age at menarche in North 24-Parganas district of West Bengal, one of the worst affected districts, and noticed that a higher mean menarcheal age of 12.50 years is reported from women residing in four arsenic-affected villages as compared to a control village (11.71 years). The differences are statistically significant ($p < 0.05$). The study indicates that arsenic exposure can delay menarcheal age (Sen and Das Chaudhudhuri, 2007).

Another research area that Prof. Sen traded into was studies on dermatoglyphics. His works included comparative studies of dermatoglyphic characteristics between two ethnic populations of North Bengal (Sen et al., 2011) and among the Limbos of Sikkim (Dorjee et al., 2015). He also published a review article on the application of dermatoglyphics in anthropological research (Dorjee et al., 2014). One of his interesting articles discussed the prediction of dental caries through dermatoglyphics (Roy and Sen, 2021). Prof. Sen, thus, showed vivid interest in so many areas of Biological Anthropology.

In all these years, Prof. Sen explored wide areas of Biological Anthropology but it seems he treasured his first interest for a long. We find him discussing trace elements again much later in 2016 (Dorjee and Sen, 2016), where they brought about the trace elements studies in nutritional anthropology. Much later, he initiated trace element studies related to the environment, mostly working on groundwater arsenic contamination in the Delta Plain of Bengal. This work was in collaboration with Prof. Bogin (Sen et al., 2021). This somewhat brought him closure to work on trace elements again and it can be well said that had he got to live his normal span of life, we would have seen him venture into trace elements and the environment furthermore.

He along with his scholar, edited a book entitled, '*Nutrition and Health among the Tribal Population of India: A Bio-Cultural Approach*' (Mondal and Sen, 2016). Another book entitled, '*Nutrition and Health among Indian Tribes: Special Reference to Eastern India*' was edited by Jyoti Ratan Ghosh and Jaydip Sen (2021), and was published after his sudden and sad demise in November 2021.

Prof. Sen continued his research until his last breath. But the teacher in him inspired us always. He was known for his good deliberations during lectures, clearing the doubts of the students, and was always accessible to them. The contents that he had written for IGNOU students, on Human Evolution, Human Variations, Growth Studies, and Nutritional Anthropology speak aloud for him.

It's heartbreaking for us to write an appraisal for a dear person like Jaydip, whose demise was a shock. Sen was recovering from COVID-19, giving a fight for almost a month, but succumbed to pneumonia. This just happened when even two days before the day he texted us about recovering and keeping well, and then everything was dark. Prof. Sen leaves behind a wide circle of close friends, relatives, his beloved companion of more than two decades, and his daughter. Sen had been to boarding school at St. Edmund's School and College in Shillong, Meghalaya and he shared many fond memories with us. About the four big playgrounds and his ever-encouraging Anglo-Indian teachers, missionary fathers who were always inspiring them to do better. His personality reflected the missionary grooming that he had. We never found him speaking ill of others or participating in any gossip about fellow people. He was gentle and a very introvert person. He was a very loving family person. He lost his father when he was pursuing his Ph.D. and he always took care of his mother. Back then, not many men enjoyed cooking or would let others know that they shared household chores. Gopa, Mithu to us is his loving wife. He had been a perfect family man and a doting father to Upasona, who is yet to come to terms with this vacuum in her life, again so early, as her father's.

Sen was a simple person with no aura around him. He was always loved and respected in the academia of Anthropology and beyond. Sen had been in the administration of the University of North Bengal for many years. He served as Controller of Examination (Acting); Superintendent of one of the boys' hostel; Convenor, Cultural sub-committee, and Coordinator of several Orientation and Refresher Courses. Even there he could keep his cool temperament as always and so his job in an appreciative way.

There's no single person who knows Sen, can bring out any negative word. That's how he was. A thorough gentleman who was always there with a smile whenever needed. We have many sweet memories during our masters, be it in the fieldwork at Ghatshila for Archaeology, supervised by Prof. A.K. Ghosh, University of Calcutta, or at Byson Hills, West Godavari district, Andhra Pradesh headed by Prof. P. K. Bhowmick, or be it during our family tour at Mirik as well. Much of the anthropological fieldwork of Bangabasi College was arranged by our friend, Jaydip, starting in 2007 at Naxalbari, Darjeeling district, and last in 2019. He loved to make the arrangements year after year and would join the teams always. Even during his last visit to Kolkata, we were in talks about planning fieldwork in an area in North Bengal, having missed out almost two years due to the Covid-created situations. None of us had the faintest idea that this would be our last conversation on the excitement of experiencing fieldwork together.

A true friend is never truly gone. Their spirit lives on in the memories of those who loved them. Jaydip will be fondly remembered by all who knew him. Friendship transcends death. Memories made will never be forgotten by those they left behind. Warmth is found through fond memories, so we curl up with them whenever we need to. Our eyes get moist, but we smile back as Jaydip would be hurt if we were sad.

Some important research contributions of Prof. Sen

Bose, A., Sinha, I., Tigga, PL., Mondal, N. and Sen, J. 2020. Socio-economic and demographic determinants of the double burden of malnutrition among Rajbanshi school-going children aged 9-14 years from North Bengal, India. *Antrocom: Online Journal of Anthropology*. 16 .2: 141-152.

Debnath, S., Mondal, N. and Sen, J. 2017. Use of upper arm anthropometry, upper arm muscle area-by-height (UAMAH), and mid-upper-arm-circumference (MUAC)-for-height as indicators of body composition and nutritional status among children. *Anthropological Review*, 80,1:85-102.

Debnath, S., Mondal, N. and Sen, J. 2018a. Socio-economic and demographic correlates of stunting and thinness among rural school-going children (aged 5-12 years) of North Bengal, Eastern India. *Journal of Life Sciences,* 10,1: 14-31.

Debnath, S., Mondal, N. and Sen, J. 2018b. Prevalence of double burden of malnutrition among Indian children. *Malnutrition: A Double Burden,* 1: 315-334.

Debnath, S., Mondal, N. and Sen, J. 2018c. Prevalence of thinness among rural children of West Bengal, India. *Human Biology Review*. 7,4: 362-385.

Debnath, S., Mondal, N. and Sen, J. 2018d. Percent of body fat, fat mass, fat-free mass and assessment of body composition among rural school-going children of Eastern India. *Anthropological Review,* 81,2:158-173.

Debnath, S., Mondal, N. and Sen, J. 2019. The double burden of malnutrition among adolescents in India. *Human Biology Review,* 8 2: 155-178.

Debnath, S. and Sen, J. 2020. Development of dermatoglyphics in India. *South Asian Anthropologist*, 20,1: 77-86.

Dorjee, B., Mondal, N. and Sen, J. 2014. Applications of dermatoglyphics in anthropological research: A review. *South Asian Anthropologist,* 14,2: 171-180.

Dorjee, B. Das, S., Mondal, N., and Sen, J. 2015. Dermatoglyphic variations among the Limbo of Sikkim, India. *HOMO*, 66,5:455-70.

Dorjee, B. and Sen, J. 2016. Trace elements, nutritional anthropology, and zinc. *South Asian Anthropologist*, 16,2:167-177.

Dorjee, B. and Sen, J. 2016. Estimation of stature from arm span, arm length, and tibial length among Bengalee children aged 3-11 years. *Human Biology Review*, 5,2: 128-145.

Dorjee, B., Bogin, B. Scheffler, C., Ghsoh, D. Sen, J. and Hermanussen, M. 2020. Association of anthropometric indices of nutritional status with growth in height among Limboo children of Sikkim, India. *Anthropologischer Anzeiger,* 77,5: 389-398.

Ghosh, JR. and Sen, J. 2021. *Nutrition and Health among Indian Tribes: Special Reference to Eastern India*. Serial Publications, New Delhi, India.

Krishan, K., Ghosh., Kanchan, T., Ngangom, C. and Sen, J. 2010. Sex differences in fingerprint ridge density causes and further observations. *Journal of Forensic and Legal Medicine,* 17,3: 172-173.

Mondal, N. and Sen, J. 2009a. Use of MUAC-for-height for the assessment of the nutritional status of rural children. *South Asian Anthropologist*, 9,2: 115-116.

Mondal N. and Sen J. 2009.Use of body mass index to assess nutritional status and health: A review of the studies done in India. *South Asian Anthropologist,* 9,1: 13-20.

Mondal, N. and Sen, J. 2010a. Prevalence of undernutrition among children (5–12 years) belonging to three communities residing in a similar habitat in North Bengal, India. *Annals of Human Biology*, 37,2: 199-217.

Mondal, N. and Sen, J. 2010b. Thinness is a major underlying problem among Indian children. *Journal of Tropical Pediatrics*, 56,6: 456-458.

Mondal, N. and Sen, J. 2010c. Prevalence of stunting and thinness among rural adolescents of Darjeeling district, West Bengal, India. *Italian Journal of Public Health*, 7,1: 54-61.

Mondal, N. and Sen, J. 2014. Role of anthropometry in the assessment of excess adiposity and metabolic disorders in Asian Indians. Public Health in 21st century: Health consequences of human central obesity.

Mondal, N., Sen, J., Bose, K., Timpungpi, R., Kathar, M. and Hanse, S. 2016. Neck circumference as a screening measure of overweight/obesity among Indian adults. *Anthropological Review*, 79,3: 347-365.

Mondal, N. and Sen, J. 2016. *Nutrition and Health among the Tribal Population of India: A Bio-Cultural Approach*, B. R. Publishing, New Delhi.

Mondal, N., Timungpi, R., Sen, J. and Bose, K. 2017a. Socio-economic and demographic correlates of overweight and obesity: A study on the Karbi women of Assam, Northeast India. *Anthropol Open J*, 2,2: 31-39.

Mondal, N., Timungpi, R., Kathar, M., Hanse, S., Teronpi, S., Timung, A., Bose, K. and Sen, J. 2017b. Cut-off point estimation of neck circumference to determine overweight and obesity among Asian Indian adults. *Epidemiology, Biostatistics, and Public Health*, 14,2:e12310-1-9.

Mondal, N., Ghosh, P. and Sen, J. 2017c. Physical growth patterns and body composition of Rajbanshi adolescent boys of Eastern India. *Human Biology Review*, 6,3: 263-283

Rengma, MS., Sen, J. and Mondal, N. 2015. Socio-economic, demographic and lifestyle determinants of overweight and obesity among adults of Northeast India. *Ethiopian Journal of Health Sciences,* 25:199-208.

Roy, S., Barman, S., Mondal, N. and Sen, J. 2016. Prevalence of stunting and thinness among adolescent girls belonging to the Rajbanshi population of West Bengal, India. *Journal of Nepal Paediatric Society,* 36,2: 147-155.

Roy, S., Pal, A., and Sen, J. 2020a. Age-specific and sex-specific variations in body composition of adults belonging to the Rajbanshi population of Darjeeling District, West Bengal, India. *Online J Health Allied Scs,* 19,4: 2.

Roy, S., Ganguly, P., Mondal, N., Krishan, and Sen, J. 2020b. Estimation of stature from hand dimensions among adult Rajbanshi individuals of Eastern India. *Journal of Indian Academy of Forensic Medicine,* 42,3: 181-188.

Roy, S. and Sen, J. 2020. Use of mid-upper arm circumference and arm-to-height ratio to estimate overweight and obesity among girls aged 5-14 years. *Antrocom: Online Journal of Anthropology,* 16,2: 283-291.

Roy, S. and Sen, J. 2021. Neck circumference as an alternative measure of central obesity among pre-hypertensive adults. *Antrocom: Online Journal of Anthropology*, 17,1: 185-196.

Roy, S. and Sen, J. 2021. Association of tri-ponderal mass index vs body mass index with mid-upper arm circumference among adolescent girls. *Journal of Nepal Paediatric Society,* 41,1: 11-16.

Roy, S. and Sen, J. 2021. Can dermatoglyphics predict dental caries? A review. *International Journal of Health and Allied Sciences*, 10,2: 95-95.

Sarkar, D. Mondal, N. and Sen, J. 2009. Obesity and blood pressure variations among the Bengali Kayastha population of North Bengal, India. *Journal of Life Sciences,* 1,1: 35-43.

Sen, J. and Daschaudhury, AB. 1995a. Trace element analysis of human hair in physical anthropology. *Journal of the Indian Anthropological Society,* 30,3: 259-268.

Sen J. and Daschaudhuri, AB. 1995b. Further studies on the relationship between hair diameter and incidence of medulla. *Journal of Human Ecology,* 6,3: 185-190.

Sen, J. and Daschaudhuri, AB. 1996a. Human hair lead and copper levels in three occupationally unexposed population groups in Calcutta. *Bulletin of Environmental Contamination and Toxicology*, 57,2: 321-326.

Sen, J. and Daschaudhuri, AB. 1996b. Hair trace element concentrations in the Bengalee population. *J Ecotoxicol Environ Monit*, 6 : 237-242.

Sen, J. and Das Chaudhuri, AB. 1997. Relationship of human hair diameter and medulla with their copper and lead concentrations. *Indian Journal of Physical Anthropology and Human Genetics,* 20,2:177-183.

Sen, J. and Daschaudhuri, AB. 2007. Effect of arsenic on the onset of menarcheal age. *Bulletin of Environmental Contamination and Toxicology,* 79,3: 293-296.

Sen, J. 2008. Contributions of biological anthropologists in assessing human exposure to toxic elements with special reference to India. *South Asian Anthropologist*, 8:103.110.

Sen, J. and Ghosh, S. 2008. Estimation of stature from foot length and foot breadth among the Rajbanshi: an indigenous population of North Bengal. *Forensic Science International,* 181,1-3: 55. e1-55. E

Sen, J. and Das Chaudhuri, AB. 2008. Arsenic exposure through drinking water and its effect on pregnancy outcome in Bengali women. *Arhiv za higijenu rada i toksikologiju,* 59,4 : 271-275.

Sen, J. 2009. Human head hair as an indicator of environmental lead exposure. *The Oriental Anthropologist,* 9,2: 255-265.

Sen, J. 2010. Human hair in personal identification and documenting drug and substance abuse. *The Anthropologist,* 12,1: 47-58.

Sen, J., Mitra, K. and Dey, S. 2010. Study on mid-upper arm circumference with special reference to under-nutrition. *South Asian Anthropologist*, 10,2: 135-145.

Sen, J., Dey, S., and Mondal, N. 2011a. Conventional nutritional indices and the composite index of anthropometric failure: Which seems more appropriate for assessing under-nutrition among children? A cross-sectional study among school children of the Bengalee Muslim population of North Bengal India. *Italian J Pub Health,* 8,2: 172-185.

Sen, J., Mondal, N., and Dey, S. 2011b. Assessment of the nutritional status of children aged 5–12 years using upper arm composition. *Annals of human biology*, 38,6: 752-759.

Sen, J., Kanchan, T. and Ghosh, A. 2011c. Sex estimation from foot dimensions in an indigenous Indian population. *Journal of Forensic Sciences,* 56: S148-S153.

Sen, J., Kanchan, T. and Mondal, N. 2011d. A comparison of palmar dermatoglyphics in two ethnic Indian populations of north Bengal, India. *Journal of Forensic Sciences*, 56,1: 109-117.

Sen, J., Mondal, N. and Dutta, S. 2013. Factors affecting overweight and obesity among urban adults: A cross-sectional study. *Epidemiology, Biostatistics, and Public Health,* 10,1: e-8741-1-11.

Sen, J. and Mondal, N. 2013. Fat mass and fat-free mass as indicators of body composition among Bengalee Muslim children. *Annals of human biology,* 40,3: 286-293.

Sen, J., Tanju, K., Ghosh, A., Mondal N. and Krishan, K. 2014. Estimation of stature from lengths of index and ring fingers in a North-eastern Indian population. *Journal of Forensic and Legal Medicine,* 22: 10-15.

Sen, J., Kanchan, T., Ghosh, A., Mondal, N., and Krishan, K. 2015b. Estimation of sex from index and ring finger lengths in an indigenous population of Eastern India. *Journal of Clinical and Diagnostic Research,* 9, HC01-HC05.

Sen, J., Mondal, N., and Ghosh, P. 2015a. Upper arm composition as an indicator of body composition and nutritional status of adolescent boys aged 10-18 years. *Journal of Nepal Paediatric Society*, 35,2: 151-160.

Sen, J., Bogin, B., Mondal, N., Dey, S. and Roy S. 2021. Groundwater arsenic contamination in the Bengal Delta Plain is an important public health issue. *Human Biology and Public Health,* 1: 1-31.

Sinha, I. and Sen, J. 2017. Factors affecting menopause among Rajbanshi women of North Bengal. *Human Biology Review,* 6,4:387-402.

Sinha, I., Mondal, N., and Sen, J. 2018. Effects of socio-economic, demographic and lifestyle variables on overweight and obesity among rural Rajbanshi post-menopausal women of India. *Anthropologischer Anzeiger*, 75,3:251-262.

Sinha, I., Tigga, PL., Mondal, N., and Sen, J. 2021. Association between age at menarche and age at menopause among women of an indigenous population of North Bengal, India. *Journal of Biosocial Science,* 53,3: 319-335.

Tigga, PL., Mondal, N. and Sen, J. 2015a. Effects of certain socio-economic, socio-demographic, and lifestyle factors on the prevalence of thinness among preschool children of North Bengal, India. *Epidemiology, Biostatistics, and Public Health.* 12: e10282-11.

Tigga, PL, Sen, J. and Mondal, N. 2015b. Association of some socio-economic variables and socio-demographic variables with wasting among preschool children of North Bengal, India. *Ethiopian Journal of Health Sciences*. 25: 63-72.

Tigga, PL., Mondal, N. and Sen, J. 2016. Head circumference as an indicator of undernutrition among tribal pre-school children aged 2-5 years of North Bengal, India. *Human Biology Review* 5,1: 17-33.

Acknowledgements

The authors acknowledge the contributions of thoughts and information on Prof. Sen, by his wife, Mrs. Gopa Sen, and our batch mate and one of our close friends, Dr Naba Kumar Duari of Anthropological Survey of India.

Index

B

C

D

E